WOMEN IN INDIA

WOMEN IN INDIA

Contemporary Concerns

Editor

U. Kalpagam

GYAN

Women in India : Contemporary Concerns

ISBN: 978-81-212-1040-6

Published in 2012 in India by
Gyan Publishing House
23, Main Ansari Road, Darya Ganj
New Delhi-110002
Phones : 23282060, 23261060
Fax : 011-23285914
E-mail: books@gyanbooks.com
Website: www.gyanbooks.com

Laser Type Setting by: Rudra Computer Graphics, Delhi
Printed at : Chawla Offset Printers, Delhi

Contents

Foreword

The articles that appear in this book were already published in a special issue of *Nivedini* November/ December 2010. One of the goals of *Nivedini* is to promote South Asian dialogue on women's issucs. Hence we thought of having country perspective feminist analysis on socio-economic and political issues within the South Asian region. We have selected India this time and hope to move on to rest of the region in South Asia. Inviting a guest editor is generally a rare occasion as the journal is regularly brought out by our organization. This is an exceptional circumstance that we thought of having a guest editor. Our choice fell on U. Kalpagam, a scholar on whose integrity and commitment to undertake this scholarly task, we had immense confidence.

The special issue having been edited by a guest editor has now taken a new turn to be brought out as a book. The volume covers a multiplicity of themes relevant to contemporary epistemology of women's studies/gender studies. The articles covered in this volume reflect many themes. Among them women's movement as the arm of academic feminism is one important aspect. As women's studies and women's movement have argued for many years, the multi-disciplinarity/inter-disciplinarity of epistemology have found vivid reflection in this collection of articles. Critical analysis of cosmology, gender and kinship within power relation of pastoral women and Muslim women's marriage contracts have brought new knowledge for us. The entry of feminist ideology into the literary field discussed in the article by Sumita Parmar is a continuing debate among many feminist literary scholars. Women studies as a discipline has challenged many traditional modes of knowledge and Kalpagam has dwelled deep into epistemology, pedagogy and politics of Women's Studies in her article.

Feminism, as we all know is embedded with radical ideas which questions accepted knowledge in many disciplines of the academia. Unfortunately, academic feminisms and women's movements have been placed dichotomously as one devaluing the other. Some feminists have pointed out that the radical ideas of feminism having been transformed into academic debates have little or no relevance to people outside the academia or the members of the women's movement. However, we as feminists and scholars disagree with such a proposition and conclude that both the movement out in the space and the academic debates within the institutions are both necessary and they both learn from each other and enrich their output as experienced epistemology. It should also be noted that feminist scholars are challenging the mainstream academia and its male bias and male chauvinistic attitudes and actions within the academic institutions. This would not have been possible if we all remain within the movement only.

Theory and practice enrich each other and teach each other in various ways. Hence, publications like this should encourage the women's movements perspective and the movement should learn from it. Experiential analysis has now become feminist methodology as positive subjectivities and is at the core of the feminist research. The academia has learnt this from the movement.

By way of acknowledgments I have to place on record the services of its editor U. Kalpagam and the publisher Gyan Publishing House for having agreed to engage with this publication very positively. In fact Gyan Publishing House has created a new space for our organization. We feel encouraged to venture into similar projects in the future.

Selvy Thiruchandran
10 May 2011
Executive Director
Women's Education and Research Centre
Colombo, Sri Lanka

Preface

A pleasant surprise awaited me when one morning in late 2009 I opened my email and found an invitation from Dr. Selvy Thiruchandran, Director of *Women's Education and Resource Centre* in Colombo, Sri Lanka to guest-edit a special issue of *Nivedini*, a reputed Journal of Gender Studies brought out by the Centre, of which she was the editor. I had seen a few issues of the journal that is now in its seventeenth year and had even published in the Journal an article of mine on women's religiosity some time ago. I was struck by the Journal's commitment to feminist internationalism, as it always had contributors and reviewers from India and elsewhere along with those from Sri Lanka. Initially I felt overwhelmed by her invitation and also of the tasks that it would entail as she firmly told me that it was a refereed journal and that it was my task of getting the papers refereed as well. After some hesitation, I accepted her offer and contacted a number of scholars who could potentially contribute to the volume. I decided to have a broad theme so that contributions from different social science disciplines could be brought together as all the disciplines are now engaged in cross-disciplinary dialogues in the interdisciplinary field of Women's Studies. I thought such an issue would interest the wide international readership of this Journal and also inform them of important on-going research in India. Although as expected, some scholars rejected my request to contribute for various reasons, I was amply encouraged by positive responses from the six scholars whose contributions appear in this book. As would be evident from the contributors' bio-data, all of them are senior and experienced scholars in Women's Studies with remarkable credentials of publications nationally and internationally. Being a journal publication, it was necessary for both contributors and referees to keep strictly to the time lines specified. A panel of referees that included both Indian and foreign scholars commented on the articles. I am thankful to Ann Kingsolver (U.S.A), Felizitas Sagebiel (Germany), Noeline Kyle (Australia), Anupama Roy, Nita Mathur, S. K.G. Sundaram and Rajnath (all from India) for exemplary roles as readers and whose comments helped the authors to revise their papers. I also offer my sincere thanks to Sita Pieris and Shanika Wijesinghe of WERC (Colombo) for copy editing and other editorial tasks. This book is therefore the outcome of an international collaborative effort. I thank Dr. Selvy Thiruchandran for giving me this opportunity and for consenting to this publication along with her Foreword for reaching a wider readership in India.

U. Kalpagam

Introduction

U. Kalpagam

Today in the era of globalization when economic and socio-cultural changes have been assuming a quickening pace with increasing transnational economic and cultural flows, and the nation-state everywhere is facing new pressures from transnational institutions and social movements, there is a need to understand the ways in which global and local forces interact and impact on women's lives in ways that challenge their traditional roles and cultural identities even as it creates new roles and identities, marginalizing some in the economic and political processes even while it opens up opportunities for others. A contemporary agenda for studies on women in India needs to further our understanding of such changes in the lives of women and to inquire if such changes enhance women's capabilities, enlarges their choice and freedom, and promotes equality and justice. The various chapters of this book written by experienced scholars and activists deal with the different issues of change and continuity in contemporary India and of the ways women of various social groups have experienced these changes.

Social scientists have long realized that the framework of socio-cultural change and continuity has always enriched societal analyses, and with the growing corpus of sociological knowledge, it has become both possible and pertinent to raise and answer new questions within this framework. A common sociological approach has been to study the impact of changes under conditions of modernity and how tradition has been retained, preserved, invented and reinvented under modernizing conditions as most societies and communities around the world came under modernizing influences through colonial and western imperialism. For the growing number of scholars engaged in women's studies whose interests have mostly been generated by their own experiences as women living in diverse cultural and political contexts, the questions of tradition and modernity and the ways it reshaped the life-worlds of women in their everyday lives became relevant to help them and other women deal with these challenges and perhaps opportunities as well. How modernity impinged on the lives of women, shaped their desires and conduct, refashioned them as modern mothers, wives, daughters and workers, expanded work opportunities, redefined private and public spheres, made them into rights-bearing citizens and modern political subjects, as also the practices and processes of inclusion and exclusion in the modernizing development process and so on have been of central concern and the staple themes of research in womens studies in post-colonial developing societies. Today, in the rapidly globalising world, these issues remain important with perhaps some renewed urgency, even as new problems posed by increasing transnational economic and cultural flows, a greater pressure on the sovereignty of nation states as a consequence of the rise of global institutions and forces, and new challenges in the realms of human development and human rights have emerged. Women's Studies has sought to understand these new challenges even as it tries to cultivate critical stances on contemporary developments from the perspective of social justice.

National independence gave many of the ex-colonial countries the opportunity to embark on national development agendas that were often if not always determined by the democratic will of the modern nation state. Even in countries where women were granted the right to vote, the political enfranchisement did not translate into the recognition of women's development needs, and the democratic will of the state represented the patriarchal interests of society. As the state began to play a central role in development, it took upon itself the task of making women into national citizens. The stakes involved for women in the citizen-making process are only recently being cognized for interpretation by scholars. That it entailed processes of inclusion of some and exclusion of others in the construction of the "national" out of the myriad ethnic and caste groupings, even as women as a group were being integrated as inferior citizens in the realms of economy, polity and society through unequal status and power. The burgeoning women's movement in post-independent India considered the state as its ally, especially since the women's movement had evolved as a response to the social reform movement and the political awakening of nationalism, and had worked in close tandem with the nationalist movement to achieve freedom from the colonial rulers. Over the years, the women's movement has placed increasing expectations and demands on the state to improve the status of women through law and development measures, even as the women's movement also acknowledged that the state could abet in women oppressive practices and hinder women's development by engaging in exclusionary politics and practices. In the last three decades of the twentieth century, the women's movement in India made significant strides in engaging with the state to secure laws in favour of women for property, dowry, domestic violence, rape, female foeticide and so on. Simultaneously, it was recognized that enhancing women's income earning capacities would secure better bargaining outcomes in patriarchal household settings. By the early nineties, the Indian state recognized the importance of women's political leadership in decentralized democratic governance and so legislated for reservation of one-third of the seats for women in the lower tiers of local governance, what are called village *panchayats* and *nagar palikas*.

At the beginning of the new millennium, the women's movement in India, which is politically heterogeneous comprising of both party-related groupings, autonomous women's groups, along with local social movements and a mushrooming number of non-governmental organizations working towards women's empowerment should have found itself as a consolidated force in the political landscape of the country. But the new challenges of neoliberal globalization brought about shifts in the perspectives and forms of political activism in the women's movement. Maitrayee Chaudhuri in her contribution in Chapter One of this book traces the shifts in the perspectives of the contemporary women's movement as a consequence of neoliberal globalization that has set two processes at work, namely a model of corporate globalization and an increasing assertion of marginalized sections. According to her, globalization is now altering the very close and uneasy relationship that Indian feminism has hitherto had with nationalism. She highlights the diverse feminist interrogations of nationalism and globalization from different vantage points. It is clear that with the institutionalization of women's movement, the radical politics and ideological moorings of the movement has been traded-off for a greater share and voice in governance with the state increasingly relying on such institutional actors to intervene in the social terrain. At the same time the state's capacity for welfare interventions have been reduced as market assumes a dominant position. As a consequence, everywhere the rights regime has enlarged which enables subaltern oppressed groups to make claims on a universal human rights basis. While gender rights are now fought on the terrain of human rights, sections of the women's movement also view the potentiality of the market to advance gender concerns. All these developments have opened up possibilities of a greater co-operation of the women's movements globally transcending to some extent the earlier alignment with nationalism.

The assertion by marginalized groups has resulted in a vibrant Dalit Women's Movement that challenges some of the assumptions of the general Women's Movement, that attempts political mobilization of all women as a group even if it recognizes the heterogeneity among women of different social classes. This assertion of Dalit women is seen both in a separate movement activism as well as a growing corpus of Dalit feminist writings expressing their experiences and the uniqueness of their oppressed existence in the caste-based society. In Chapter Two, Fatima Burnard Nadesan writes on the Dalit Women's Movements in Tamil Nadu highlighting the social discrimination, economic deprivation and the everyday violence experienced by Dalits in the state that is also much the same elsewhere in the country as well. Dalit Women's Movements in the state, of which she has been both an initiator and active participant for over three decades, has sought to act against atrocities on Dalit women and bring justice in numerous instances of violence against Dalit women as well as men. They have also taken up the issue of securing land rights to Dalit women. The Dalit movement in the country has sought to place their issues in international forums as a human rights case of racial discrimination. Although it is heartening to note that the Dalit Women's Movement is active in the state of Tamil Nadu and elsewhere, it raises an important issue of why Dalit Women's Movement need to be separate and different from other Women's Movements. Quite obviously, Dalit women most likely feel that their experience of humiliation and oppression being a consequence of hierarchical social structure of power and privilege in a caste society would require a radical transformation of societal relations which the general women's movements may not be adequately cognizing and acting upon. In terms of efficiency and effectiveness, issue-based mobilization and struggle of those affected are also likely to be more effective. The Dalit Women's Movements are an integral part of the women's movements in the country requiring both solidarity and collaborative actions around numerous issues.

With the institutionalisation of the Women's Movement in the country, many actors and stake–

holders are claiming voice in governance issues as a way to express the collective agency of women in shaping state policies and bureaucratic interventions in the domain of development and poverty alleviation. Its importance is being increasingly recognized as a strategy of gender empowerment. The experience with several poverty alleviation programmes in the 1970s and 1980s, such as the Integrated Rural Development Programme, highlighted the fact of leakages in the delivery of services through corruption and the siphoning of benefits by the non-intended beneficiary classes. In all assessments, it became clear that poor women and women-headed households fared badly in terms of access to and benefits from services. In the present context of neoliberal globalisation, governance and democracy need to be strengthened as the market mechanisms of neoliberal growth are likely to further marginalize the weak players on the market. Thus issues of transparency, accountability, and right to information from the state have assumed crucial importance in enlarging the sphere of people's participation in democratic governance and rights-based development.

The period of structural adjustment since the 1990s in different countries globally has clearly highlighted how macro-economic forces impinge on women employment, incomes and their lives. Women in India and elsewhere have been demanding transparency and accountability in the state's budgetary process as resource transfers by the state are important for mainstreaming women in the development process. In Chapter Three, Vibhuti Patel examines the process of gender budgeting and gender audit and its consequences for resource allocation for development schemes that impact on poor women's lives. Gender budgeting is concerned with ensuring that adequate budgetary allocations are made for programmes that benefit women, enhance their capabilities and resource entitlements. Gender audit is a form of social audit that ensures that the money spent has reached and benefited the target groups. It is therefore an audit that proceeds from the grassroots to the higher echelons of the bureaucracy. Such gender and social audits are increasingly being demanded by civil society organizations. The mammoth National Rural Employment Guarantee Scheme that was launched in 2004 and progressively expanded sought to build such gender and social audit on a large-scale that was hitherto neither envisaged nor practised. Even if the market becomes increasingly important, the state has a significant role in the empowerment of poor women in developing countries.

Whatever be the nature of societal changes, the one institution that has been crucial to women's lives and experiences has been the family. The family undergoes changes not merely from the joint to the nuclear family but also in terms of how social organization, whether feudalism or capitalism, structures and integrates the family and kinship relations within social modes of production and reproduction. Changes in the family also encompasses changes in norms, values, behaviors and practices within families in terms of intergenerational and gender relations as society modernizes and new opportunities in various realms open up. More recently, gay, lesbian and transgender groups have challenged the notion of the family based on heterosexual union with more diversity in domestic unions and arrangements with increasing legal sanction. Despite such changes the family remains central in women's lives shaping their conduct, desires, behaviours, identities and experiences. Life experiences of women, both favourable and unfavourable, are often the outcome of power relations that use emotional and material resources in negotiating in familial contexts and relations. It is therefore not surprising that the family still continues to be one of the central themes of fiction and films everywhere. The diversity of themes and perspectives in the fiction on family everywhere reflects the diversities in cultural differences as well as the differences in the experiences themselves. Such differences preclude any meta-narrative about the family as being an oppressive institution or otherwise, as the different experiences testify. Yet being the primary site of socialization of women and girls, its role in the construction of femininity and masculinity and of gendered identities has to be cognized in explanations of women's subordinate status and patriarchy in general.

In Chapter Four, Sumita Parmar reflects in her essay on how the family has figured as a recurring theme in the fictional novels of Shashi Deshpande, a well-known contemporary Indian woman writer. What emerges from her analysis are the ways in which the writer persuades the reader through the narrative plotting of her fiction that women in familial contexts could exercise significant agency to refashion their selves as autonomous beings. While it is very relevant to reinforce the myriad possibilities of individual agency to most middle class educated women, whom I suppose are the constituency of readers of Shashi Deshpande and in fact some of whom may be feeling helpless in certain familial contexts, the women's movements all over have for long pointed to the insufficiency of individual agency for changing gender power structures in society. Yet building capacities of women to exercise agency in everyday contexts of familial life is very important. Even if the Women's Movement gets the state to pass a law on men sharing the burden of household chores, it is really the women in the family who can ensure that such sharing does in fact take place.

Anthropologists have often felt that feminist scholars tend to have reified notions of the family especially when they analyse patriarchal power relations in the family. They have produced a corpus of ethnographic knowledge on the cultural variability in sex-gender systems and gender roles thereby challenging universalist notions of patriarchal family structures. Yet others have pointed out that in the process of social change, many societies have shown tendencies towards the institution of such patriarchal family structures. Chapter Five by Subhadra Channa provides much food for thought on these issues. In her engaging ethnographic study of the Jad Bhotiya women who reside in the upper reaches of the Himalayan mountains, she has observed that the external forces that affected their society are that they have since the 1960s period of Tibetan conquest been compelled to stop their long standing trade with Tibetan communities and have been forced to move to the lower ranges of the mountain region. This brought them increasingly under the influence of both the dominant Hindu ideology of the north Indian plains people even as the nation-state sought to integrate them into the mainstream through its development strategies. This she notes, has brought slow but perceptible changes in the lives of the Jad Bhotiya women whose cosmology, kinship and marriage practices are vastly different from the Hindu culture.

Jad Bhotiya women enjoyed far greater autonomy and freedom as they have not been restricted by mothering roles, as children are perceived as the responsibility of the entire community. She explores how the Hindu influence is progressively subordinating these women as Jad society imbibes the Hindu patriarchal attitudes and practices.

Law has been considered the harbinger of modern social change in India and other developing societies. The pace of change of traditional institutions such as marriage can be hastened by modern law. Modern law in liberal societies constructs modern individuals on the basis of equality and liberty, even if their conditions of social existence are neither fully equal nor free. It is by now well known that modern law was introduced in India under colonial rule. However, different religious communities in India are governed by different personal laws as regard marriage, divorce and inheritance. Attempts to introduce a Uniform Civil Code that was on the agenda of the Women's Movement in the eighties have now been put on the back burner as it generated a massive protest of Muslim identity politics based on what has since become the famous 'Shah Bano case'. Since then it was felt that reform in personal laws and practices should be initiated from within the various communities themselves. Chapter Six by Rehana Ghadially deals with recent attempts within the Indian Muslim communities to evolve a consensus-based standardized *Nikhanama* (the written marriage contract) for the different Muslim groups and of how Muslim women's groups entered into the debate and produced their own revised version of the contract that they believed was far more accommodative of women's interests and concerns than the other attempts at revision that were initiated by the Muslim clergy and the Muslim elders. Although Muslim women's status cannot be improved merely through the revision of the marriage contract, Muslim women have considered such revisions as necessary in many other Islamic societies as well. This chapter once again confirms that there are multiple and intersecting patriarchies that structure groups and communities, and that there it needs to be particular kinds of mobilization to dismantle or change such patriarchies in different communities. It is therefore not surprising that there is an emerging Muslim Women's Movement in the country much like the Dalit Women's Movement which is indeed separate but does align with the women's movements in general.

Women's Studies in India and elsewhere have produced a vast and growing knowledge on women and gender relations in society. Feminist scholars have also reflected on the conditions of the possibility of producing such knowledge, and the process of validation of such knowledge especially as such knowledge is sought to be based on women's experiences. There have been many debates in Western philosophy on the role of experience in constructing knowledge, and feminist scholars have questioned male bias in the production of scientific knowledge. One needs to bear in mind that such knowledge is not produced for the sake of knowledge but is geared to bringing social transformations oriented to equality and justice for women. It is to the credit of the communities of feminist scholars and activists worldwide that they have normalized this cycle of knowledge production, activism based on such knowledge, and pedagogical practices to generate better knowledge on a continuing basis, as an essential feature of modern developing societies. In

Chapter Seven U. Kalpagam discusses issues pertaining to the above in the Indian context and argues the central role of women's experiences in frameworks of feminist epistemology, pedagogical practices and the political role of Women' Studies to advance women's concerns of justice, equality and peace.

It would be evident from the chapters that follow that there are various contemporary concerns for women in India in the domains of polity, economy and society. New problems and perspectives have arisen in the context of contemporary globalization which the women's movements in the country are actively engaged with. It is also evident that studies on women would continue to be a vibrant and enriching feature of social science in the country.

1

Nationalism is Not What it Used to be, can Feminism be any Different? A View from India

Maitrayee Chaudhury

This chapter seeks to examine some of the new challenges that face democratic movements in general and the women's movement in particular in the context of globalization. The vantage-point from which it seeks to do so is the idea and practice of nationalism and of the nation state in India. There are a couple of reasons for doing so: (i) The history of the Indian national movement and the women's movement have intersected at many points, diverged and contested in many others. If indeed, we are faced with a post-national condition as some have argued, how are we to now conceive of either the nation or the state or the women's movement?

(ii) Given the close linkages between Indian nationalism and the Indian nation state with the women's movement, it is not surprising that there is an important and rich body of Indian feminist scholarship on the idea of the Indian nation and Indian womanhood. Much of this critique has veered around the gendered and caste nature of the cultural representations of the nation and of women. The political economy of nationalism retreated even as the hegemonic nature of Indian nationalism and the Indian state featured in feminist scholarship. The challenges of globalization have perforce brought back an overt engagement with questions of political economy. This engagement often comes from unexpected quarters: sections within the Dalit and feminist movement on the one hand and from proponents of globalization on the other. How does this help us understand gender and its connection with nationalism and the state in a globalizing context? (iii) New critiques of nationalism particularly within the Dalit movement have emerged. This has been accompanied by a linked rethinking of British colonialism against which Indian nationalism arose. Significantly such rethinking is not confined to a section within the Dalit movement but has been echoed in quite another quarter by the Indian Prime Minister Manmohan Singh who articulated a new assessment of British colonialism at a talk at his alma mater, the University of Oxford. It is not beside the point therefore to recall that Manmohan Singh is widely perceived as the architect of India's present tryst with globalization. How do we read this congruence?

My contention in this chapter is that any effort to address the above questions demands an analysis of the transformed structures of power in contemporary India.

I argue that the key to understanding this transformed structure are two disparate developments that together and at once impinge on the structural and ideological formations of contemporary India. One pertains to the assertions of subaltern groups, the other to the changing nature of capital. While the first interrogates the exclusive and hegemonic character of the 'nation state' the other seeks to redefine a national order more in sync with the imperatives of global capital and a now transnational Indian capitalist class. This would help us fully appreciate why neither nationalism nor feminism nor the state is not quite what it used to be.

These two social forces are constitutive of each other but with different pasts and different trajectories. The first pertains to the dynamics of contemporary India, the assertions of dalits, backward classes, tribals, religious communities that can be read also as a fall-out of the intended and unintended measures of the 'national' and 'developmental state'. Sixty years of affirmative action, land reforms and green revolution have led to new middle classes and powerful middle castes. If this be read as success then the failure would be the large sections who have not been able to avail of any benefits of 'development' but have been 'victims' of development, displaced off land, home and livelihood. The second pertains to the far reaching changes initiated by a neoliberal globalization which have ushered in momentous social changes, a growing middle class and an altered public discourse. But importantly it has had its own consequences for the aforementioned local movements with its own internal dynamics. The Dalit movement and an increasingly visible Dalit diaspora would thus rally globally to ensure that the Durban Conference recognize dalits as victims of racial discrimination. International institutions would play no mean role in this (Lerche 2008). Likewise the tribal movement in India would have stakes in being recognized by the Indian state and globally as indigenous people. This connection between the local/national and global is of course nothing new. The story of the Indian national movement with its diverse linkages with an international anti-imperial movement is only one of the many obvious cases. The women's movement in India similarly has had close links in the colonial period to global movements. In 1975, the Declaration of the International Women's Decade by the United Nations was in many ways a marker for it began a period of institutionalization of the women's movement and women's studies. And it is this matter of institutionalization which I would like to argue alters the nature of the linkages between the global and the national.

I argue that while ideas and movements in the modern period have often crossed borders, never more than the period of colonialism and the heydays of liberalism, socialism and nationalism, *what has altered has been a concerted move to harness social movements by both states and international agencies.* A quick reference to India's tenth Five Year Plan may be in order here. With, 'the acceptance of market liberalism and globalization', India's Tenth Five Year Plan (2002-2007) document states how "it is expected that the state yields to the market and the civil society in many areas where it, had a direct but distortionary and inefficient presence...It also includes the role of the state as a development catalyst where, perhaps, civil society has better institutional capacity. At the same time, with the growth of markets and the presence of an aware and sensitive civil society, many developmental functions as well as functions that provide stability to the social order have to be progressively performed by the market and civil society organizations" (2002:181). Both the state and international institutions as we shall shortly see envisioned what I would like to call an institutionalized role for social movements and civil society organizations. Poor women as both agents and recipients of development fit very well into this scheme of things.

The term *institutionalization* is widely used in social theory to denote the process of making something become embedded within an organization, social system, or society as an established custom or norm or within that system. If the Tenth Plan document referred above is an indication, quite clearly the state saw in social movements a partner rather than an antagonist. It is also reasonably certain that not all political movements would be seen in such light which bring us to the question of the nature of a social movement or even that of a social organization. Some would be more amenable to a partnership, some less.

At this point, I would like to make a distinction between the nature and mode of institutionalization itself. One agrees with the contention that in the case of peasant movements (and the argument could very well be extended to all social movements) "there has been the processes of transformation of social movements from that of the intensive phase of radical action to institutionalization" (Singha Roy 2005). What this paper would like to focus upon however is *not* the general process of routinization but the *large scale and specific form of institutionalization of civil society organizations and social movements by the state, by international institutions (IIs), by non governmental organizations (NGOs) and importantly by the corporate sector that has been underway with globalization.* To give but just one instance is the link made between women's reproductive health and population stabilization, made explicit in the Cairo Conference, reaffirmed in the Beijing Conference and now mainstay of developmental strategies, part of the given working knowledge which states, NGOs and research institutions function with (Dube and Jabbi 2009). Likewise the manner that micro credit has come to be the buzzword for women's development, equally at home among grass root organizations, corporate boardrooms, finance ministries and major banks.

This matter of institutionalization is further compounded by what would be the logic of professionalization of social movements and research institutions, even when committed to action research. There would be funding protocols, agendas, targets, standard modes of evaluation for projects built in, which over time would necessarily alter the manner of functioning, whatever be the original intent. As academics, one increasingly encounters a sense of being rapidly converted into service providers, not very different from the wide range of civil society organizations (Chaudhuri, 2010). There is an increasing impression that research necessarily means evaluations (Krishnaraj, 2005). And such research alone can be useful. Both the content and form of the ongoing process of institutionalization has a tangible impact on the practice and theory of feminism. And that this altered pattern of institutionalization is our key to understand what is it that is redefining nationalism and the manner in which the state functions today.

The implications of institutionalization on social movements, NGOs and the academia are profound. One gets trained to work within given guidelines. Questions outside either cease to arise or if they do, tend to get dumped as irrelevant, impractical and meaningless. The entire task of researchers and project executives become that of technicians and managers. The agenda is taken as given. It is in this context that I find it particularly useful to return to some core aspects of institutions.

> Institutions are the foundations of social life. *They consist of formal and informal rules, monitoring and enforcement mechanisms, and systems of meaning that define the context* within which individuals, corporations, labour unions, nation states and other organizations operate and interact with each other. (Cambell 2004:1)

To recapitulate my central contention, there are two forces at work: one, a model of corporate globalization, and two, increasing assertions of marginalized sections which perforce raise new issues and new ways of thinking them. Further, while the latter has very deep local/national antecedents, globalization (both the corporate model and the global civil society one) has impinged on both, their content and mode of functioning. And further still, a distinct logic of institutionalization through the state, through the IIs, through NGOs, through new practices in the academia is at work redefining both nationalism and feminism. This perforce has to take into account the changing dynamics of capitalism and the interests of capitalists to invest and profit from anywhere in the world sans territorial/ national restrictions. Indian capitalists have been particularly adventurous in global acquisitions. If they no longer have stakes in economic nationalism, nor do dalits nor do women nor the poor, has been one line of argument.

The *structure of this chapter* would roughly correspond to the manner that I have articulated my argument. Feminism has had a very close and also a very uneasy relationship with nationalism. The chapter veers around this. In part II, I begin with a very discernable and once dominant strand within the Indian women's movement which saw its goal as inextricably linked to the nationalist project. And move on to the diverse feminist interrogations of colonialism, nationalism and globalization from very different locations. This as the next section would show is of great relevance to contemporary response to globalization. Part III therefore looks at *two* broad responses to both the nationalist framework and the globalization model from within the women's movement: *one* discerns clear possibilities in globalization, the *other* a loss. I seek to analyse also the convergence of positions between pro-globalizers and a section of the dalit movement and strands within feminist articulations. In conclusion part IV returns to my key contention that contemporary India witnesses a fusion of the dynamics of a globalizing India, with its Brand nationalism and 'corporate feminism' on the one hand and concerns of social movements on the other. In the dominant discourse of civil society the appropriation is tangible.

II

The Nationalist Framework, Feminist Linkages and Interrogations

Early scholarship on gender in India often highlighted how "feminism and nationalism were closely inter-linked". The "goal of independence became the only concern for both men and women" (Basu 1976:40). Likewise as the narrative of a pioneer of women studies in India, Vina Mazumdar suggests, "the independence of the country and of women had become so intertwined as to be identical." What had been mainly an individual women's effort at 'managing' the demand of professional and family responsibilities, changed into a collective and ideological struggle for *rediscovery of the nation*, the world, the past, the present and the future- *from the perspective of India's hidden and unacknowledged majority, i.e. poor working women in rural and urban areas* (Mazumdar 2001:135 emphasis mine). Poor women as icons of the nation were one way of imagining the nation with obvious implications for nation building. The independent nation state saw as one of its central task an effort to address itself to their needs. That this vision of the poor could be faulted as largely caste blind is a matter that is being increasingly raised by the women's and dalit movement.

The first Plan Document on women, one of the twenty nine subcommittees set up by the National Planning Committee (NPC) 1938, titled significant as *Women's Role in a Planned Economy* (WRPE), therefore did highlight women workers, both urban and rural. But the logic of the developmental model that was adopted was unable to address them (Chaudhuri 1996). It was not long before the language of women's welfare overrode that of women's and worker's rights. The 1950s and 60s saw the re-emergence of "women" in the community development programmes (financed by the Ford Foundation) whose projects were geared to enable village women to become, in the words of the director of the Women's programme in 1959, "a good wife, a wise mother, a competent housewife and a responsible member of the village community". Women's work and labour are not alluded to (John 1996 note 6).

A question often raised is how did the left oriented WRPE completely disappear from public discourse on development and gender in independent India? Why did transformation of gender relationships disappear when the other aspects pertaining to social equity and state planning, characteristic of WRPE persist? I offer two sets of explanations. One that is specific to gender. There was a clear retreat from a more radical questionings of sexualities and sexual division of labour of an earlier period to a time when the Hindu Code Bill was being opposed not just by conservatives but by many within the Indian Nationalist Congress (Chaudhuri, 1993). Significantly one should recall that much of the 19th century middle class social reform were self consciously seeking to refashion the family in an ideal typical modern, western bourgeois family with a male breadwinner and a domesticated genteel mother and wife (Sangari and Vaid 1989, Chaudhuri 1993). The challenge clearly stemmed from a patriarchal notion of social order, identity and tradition, heightened in the aftermath of unprecedented violence of partition. A committee for Abducted Women was formed and feminist scholars have etched out from the tragic narratives how the women's voices were violently brushed aside before the decisions of the state and nation (Butalia 1998, Menon and Bhasin 1998). This period also marked the confrontation of the Nehruvian Congress government and the Communists with the Tebhaga and Telengana Peasant Movement. And a little later by the 1962 war with China. Recalling the historic peasant movements are important for it brings to the fore the conflicts, glossed over today, that the nationalist framework did face. Relevant to this chapter is also the fact that a section of the communist movement read the nationalist framework as one that belied the 'freedom' that people fought for. It would be interesting to compare the present dalit critique and the old left one of a nationalist framework that necessarily marginalized the subaltern.

A point that this chapter seeks to communicate is that it is important to simultaneously analyze both the local/national and international context. For at one level a great deal of maneuverings of the state often happen vis a vis strategic moves with a global order that had its own objectives. Locating the Community Development Programmes in a Cold War era India is not inappropriate (Singh1986: 9-10). Indeed, in the contemporary period I argue that Women Studies can provide a vantage-point to understand these moves of global politics and dominant global frames of development, be it in the rapid growth of microcredit and selffinance groups or in shifts in higher education policies or in new discourses of choice and autonomy. Indeed often violent interventions have been defended on the grounds that it was liberating for women.

If one were to identify a core critique of the nationalist framework from the rich body of Indian feminist scholarship and the women's movement, it would be the tendency of a nationalist framework to conflate the dominant group with the nation and state. A great deal of feminist theorizing in India, therefore, has interrogated the imagining of a nation that conflated itself with a sanitized image of upper caste women. While writing on modern India has explored the recasting of women in colonial India (Sangari and Vaid

1989; Chaudhuri 1993; Uberoi 1996), scholars of ancient India have interrogated the Altekarian vision of the high and noble status of women in ancient India (Chakravarti 1989; Roy 1996).

One of the more significant critiques in recent years has been that by the Dalit movement and scholarship. As V. Geetha puts it, a visit to the past is imperative for the progress or retardation of the women's movement in India. But "such an less understanding cannot merely veer between the elite and subaltern versions of Indian nationalism, but would have to actively engage with the histories and ideologies of social and political movements whose founding premises were not, in fact, are not definable within the terms of Indian nationalism" (V. Geetha 2004:156). In a similar vein Sharmila Rege observes that the non-brahmanical re-constructions of historiography of modern India...have underlined the histories of anti-hierarchical, pro-democratising collective aspirations of the lower caste masses which are not easily encapsulated within the histories of anti-colonial nationalism" (Rege 1998).

In fact these histories, Rege contends, have often faced the penalty of being labeled as collaborative. But dalit interrogations are quite clearly not the only ones for new narratives of nationalism. Prime Minister Manmohan Singh, when he spoke of the benefits of colonialism for a modern Indian nation, clearly was engaging in reframing nationalist history for global capitalism which surely would require new global histories just as nationalism did. At this point of time, global histories are being re-written on two registers:

one of global capital and the other of the previously marginalized and excluded. And on occasions they coalesce. But on occasions they do not (Patnaik 2005, Gopal Guru 2005).

III

Adverse Nationalism, Advantageous Globalization or the other way Around

I argue that there are two very distinct locations from which a pro-globalization position is being articulated: one from within social movements, whether dalit, women, or political left; and two, from the self conscious ideological adherents of neo-liberalism itself as well as from the beneficiaries of the process itself. We start with the first set and look at the views strongly articulated by the Dalit movement. The Durban Conference was the first big event. Many other global initiatives have been taking place. To mention but one, a concurrent bill was introduced at the 110th American Congress Session on caste and untouchability. It was then referred to the Congress Committee on Foreign Affairs. And as I write the debate about caste as race has hit headlines again. I am tempted to quote for it brings back to the fore the crisscrossing of issues, the significance of global agenda and the persistence of nation and the state. The review of the World Conference on Racism (WCAR), which addressed the issues of "racism, racial discrimination, xenophobia and related intolerance," states:

> India is also fighting a related battle, of giving tribals the status of "indigenous people". For India, this is unacceptable because this could open a can of worms that would be uncontrollable.

> *Given the huge presence and profile of NGOs in global human rights discourse, India can expect a battering from organizations like Human rights Watch, international Dalit organization etc. Analysts of the UN process said these little inclusions in official documents make a big difference on the field- in terms of funding to social activists organizations. This could be channeled to organizations with a strong caste basis (TOI,* 18th April 2009).

Evident in the debate about racial discrimination is the fact that sections within the Dalit movement understand the nationalist framework as limiting and globalization as a historical point where the dalit can have access to capital, and become players in the game. For as Chandra Bhan Prasad argues, "Dalits have no stake in India's wealth but are expected by 'progressives to protect India's wealth and business interests from the forces of imperialism' (Prasad 2002). Kancha Illaiah makes a distinction between economic and cultural globalization, arguing that while the former has created "a nightmarish" situation for the poor, cultural globalization has opened up "a new channel of hope for historically suppressed masses". While the nationalist framework post colonialism had imposed a Brahmanic culture denigrating the productive culture of the Dalit Bahujans, globalization has reopened "channels" to integrate global culture with this productive culture (Illaiah 2003). It is significant that in the nationalist framework women figured significantly as cultural emblems. This 'national culture' both dalit and feminist critique would see as both hegemonic and exclusive.

Gail Omvedt from a Marxist Dalit position contends that "being anti-globalisation" has become the correct standard of political correctness (Omvedt 2005). She agrees with Rohini Hensman who argues that in a globalised world "if capitalism is acting as midwife at the birth of a borderless world, shouldn't we be ready to nurture the new arrival and imbue it with our values of justice and love instead of trying to push it back into the womb of history?" (Hensman 2004:1030). She wonders, "Why is there such a passionate opposition to the undermining of national borders? 'Imperialism and its world war' grew organically out of European nationalism. Chandra Bhan's clear stance that 'we want a bourgeoisie to emerge from the dalits for "without a dalit bourgeoise, dalits can hardly claim total emancipation', (Prasad 2002). Omvedt argues in a similar vein that "the only meaningful question is, for a Marxist (or dalit, or feminist) activist, what advances the revolution, that is, the movement towards a non-caste, non-patriarchal, equalitarian and sustainable socialist society?" (Omvedt 2005: 4881).

But Omvedt's and Hensman's ideological grounds are not the only ones upon which possibilities are discerned in globalization. There is quite another generation and quite another stance. One had mentioned at an earlier point the iconic nation of the poor and dispossessed in various strands of both nationalism and feminism in India. An Omvedt, a Hensman, a Mazumdar with sharply variegated stances vis-a-vis nationalism veer around the centrality of the poor in their political visions. In some feminist articulations today a break emerges with that vision, whether of a socialist feminist kind or of a nationalist feminist one. Scholars have argued the grounds on which feminists are sharply divided about their relationship to the state (Sunder Rajan 2003).

India, in 1997, had witnessed protests by the women's movement against beauty contests on the grounds that "these contests both glorify the objectification of women and serve to obscure the links between consumerism and liberalisation in a post-globalization economy". Processions were held in Bangalore with mock 'queens' crowned as 'Miss Disease', 'Miss Starvation', 'Miss Poverty', 'Miss Malnourished', 'Miss Dowry Victim', etc. in order to *highlight the issues of poverty*, and lack of nutrition and health care in the country (Phadke 2003: 4573). Shilpa Phadke argues in this context that 'the focus on women as 'victims' could well serve to erase images of women as subjects with agency, sometimes suggesting that *feminism is a movement devoid of joy*'. She further notes that 'the contestants' insistence on the voluntary nature of their participation was ignored by women's groups' and they were seen inevitably as 'victims in the thrall of a false consciousness'. '*Not only did the context and content of the arguments made by women's groups serve to deny agency to the contestants*, they also could not contribute to addressing *the increasing aspirations and anxieties built around the desire for beauty or sexual success*' (Phadke 2003:4573 emphasis mine). The nation and women's own aspirations and sexualities were posited as opposed, quite dramatically in contrast to the positions articulated by Mazumdar. Phadke further contends that 'the women's movement critiques of the 1997 Miss World Contest in India could potentially be read as an effort located in the protecticn of the nation conceived in terms of desexualised womanhood'. Phadke's break from the past does not stop with the necessary and happy break between 'nationalism and feminism'. She argues that the market rather than the state is better as 'a potential turf for negotiation.' For "unlike the state, where the citizen is largely a client, for the market the individual is first and foremost an actor-consumer. Can the women's movement use the strategies of the market to re-sell itself to a larger audience and reclaim its right to speak on behalf of a larger constituency of women? Can we reclaim the language of choice and restore its radical edge?" (ibid 4575).

Not all would agree with the contention about the market as an "actor consumer". The idea of citizenship as both hegemonic and potentially liberating has been argued time and again (Roy 2005). Many Indians persist with the idea of a benevolent Leviathan chartered to bring about growth or to eliminate poverty. Neera Chandoke drawing evidence from a survey found that most respondents continued to perceive the state and political parties rather than the market or NGOs as responsible for their "basic needs" and they approached either the government agency concerned or political parties when they needed resolution of any problem (Chandoke 2005). In another context in the immediate aftermath of the Mumbai terrorist attack of November 2008, Indian media witnessed unprecedented bashing of the state and political parties by the well heeled, there was just one gentle reminder that while the great Indian middle class may not need the government, the vast majority of the poor do. More recently and readers would note that this is after the global meltdown, there has been write ups welcoming the 'corporate take over'. The newspaper feature cited below, is written in the context that the IPL cricket matches were asked to be rescheduled in the light of the 2009 General Elections in India. The IPL owners decided to shift the venue to South Africa.

> ... *As India globalises, it has to become a little more accountable to the rest of the world.* For instance Tata Motors has foreign investors too who wants to see action...The public is learning its lessons. It's cocking a snook now, with the corporate sector taking the lead. Our politicians couldn't provide leadership, so these business leaders are taking the helm... They are not just businessman. They are *social reformers*...the Indian economy... grows at night, because the government is sleeping then. By not letting the state come in the way of customer service, these businessmen are setting a new credo: *Despite the state*, I will serve you and meet the commitments made (Varma 2009 emphasis mine).

I cannot enter here into the recent scandal around IPL 2010 that hit both the state and the corporate world.

The key contention around which this Chapter is framed is the importance to appreciate the contemporary juncture as one that contains both the top down dynamics of globalization and the bottom up dynamics of grassroots organizations, many (not all) which have also liberally dipped into the language of international institutions and sometimes into neoliberal discourse itself. And feminism in India reflects in its diversity all of that but also intellectual orientations that is steeped in academic orientations dominant in North America with its repertoire of feminist concerns.

If there are voices that see globalization as progressive, many within the women's movement are not just uneasy but distinctly critical. A quick way to focus on this is by addressing how the informal sector is looked at, given that in the neo-liberal framework it is the heart of the market econcmy and represents its prime model (Kalpagam 1994). Feminist scholars were quick to indicate the manner that the new model was appropriating feminist findings and deploying it for its own use. One of the crucial texts to come out of the subsequent decade of the 1980s was the *Shramshakti* report on self employed women and women in the informal sector that was published in 1988. The *World Bank Gender and Poverty Report* followed only a few years later. It focused on "the incredible range of tasks poor women perform, their often greater contribution to household income despite lower wage earnings, their ability to make scarce resources stretch further under deteriorating conditions..." But a crucial shift in signification takes place, "these findings are no longer arguments about *exploitation* so as much as proofs of *efficiency*" (John 1996). So the 'poor', once the icon of Indian nationalism reappear in a new avatar.

Given the centrality of this model, a great deal of development gender discourse is now exclusively addressed within the micro-credit framework, premised upon the idea that women are efficient managers and can be trusted to repay. The rationale of micro-credit is based on the hypothesis that the poor can be relied upon to return on time the money that they borrow. The poor are encouraged to save and practice thrift while the growing body of middle class Indian women are encouraged to spend (Chaudhuri 1998, 2001). In the discourse of micro-credit and self-help groups, the categories of class and production relations disappear. The 'poor' and 'poverty' appear to be self-contained entities with no structural connect with production relations. Naila Kabeer argues that it is the "imperatives of cost-recovery and financial sustainability which drive the financial systems approach clearly resonate neo-liberal orientation to market principles" and that "it is not surprising therefore that it has come to assume a hegemonic position in international development thinking about micro-finance as a tool for poverty reduction" (Kabeer 2005:4709).

The political implications of making the informal sector, where the greater proportion of women workers are, the hub of the new economy is as Breman argues:

> ...the informalisation of gainful employment which has become a major trend especially in developing countries in this late phase of capitalism hampers steady increase in the wretchedly low wages and regular employment with casual, spasmodic work arrangements, paid not in time-based wages but on piece rates. *An economic regime of this kind discourages militancy and obstructs the mobilization of the labouring poor into other unions and other representative organizations* (Breman 2004:3872 emphasis mine).

In this above unwieldy account of responses to globalization there appears little that holds it together. If Breman speaks of the obstructing logic of flexible labour on possibilities of collective struggles, others speak of the immense possibilities that globalization ushers in. One can hazard the claim that there has been a shift from a language of liberation to a language of stakes.

Many registers removed from the debate on the working class and dalit woman are moves by the corporate sector to operationalize feminist concerns. Often today the nation itself is referred to as India

Incorporated or Brand India and there has been an incredible move towards corporatization in all spheres including that of the academia and other centres of knowledge production. Advertisements and sponsorships have played a huge role in redefining dominant public discourse. The very term 'feminism' has undergone a shift that moves it away from a collective emancipatory project to a lifestyle statement of choices (Chaudhuri 2000).

There are other moves within the corporate sector to implement what they perceive more gender friendly work space. An example of what could be described as corporatization of gender rights would be the advertisement that I refer to below from the January 2008 issue of the magazine *India Today Woman...* A two full page advertisement with three shelves of shoes, placed at some distance (space) from each other, has a brief write up titled as *Match Point*.

> *Gender inclusivity aims at creating work spaces to entice a college graduate, a career woman and a mother.* Recognizing this change, Nasscom and *India Today Woman* announced winners of the corporate awards for *Excellence in Gender Inclusivity*, recognizing companies that have implemented outstanding practices in promoting gender empowerment (India Today Woman, 2008, emphasis mine).

Another small advertisement may help us further appreciate gender in the corporate vision. This is about a Workshop on Work-life Balance for Working Women in Delhi.

> *Across generations, gender, industries, and international borders, work-life balance is surfacing as a common concern.* What is the high price of a life that is out of balance? Within the past decade or so, *the global workplace* has seen increased numbers of working women; dual-career and single parent families, and increased numbers of employees with eldercare responsibilities; a decrease in job security; and a blurring of work-family boundaries due to technological change.

What we see at work above are two sets of assertions. One, that of an upwardly mobile middle class, two, that of women from a certain section within the corporate sector. What is also discernible is a model of 'fulfilling life', a 'balanced life' and of course a more obvious affirmation of the new individuated self. Many issues raised by women's movements and women's studies have indeed entered public discourse and the new everyday commonsense. On occasions we have a crasser version of how gender has traveled in public discourse. For instance a case was registered against a leading telecom firm under the Pre-Natal Diagnostic Techniques (Prohibition of Sex Selection) Act for 'displaying an advertisement on its website pertaining to sex determination of the foetus with a suggestive 'Better Rs. 500 now than Rs. 5 lakh later 'message (*HT* Feb 1 2005).

IV

In Conclusion: the logic of doing the 'doable'

I have argued at the outset that we need to locate some of the recent developments in two contexts, increasingly constitutive of each other, but in many ways with different pasts and different trajectories. The *first* pertains to the dynamics of contemporary India, the assertions of dalits, backward classes, tribals, religious communities that can be read also as a fall-out of the intended and unintended measures of the 'national' and 'developmental state'. The *second* to the far reaching changes initiated by a neoliberal globalization which have ushered in momentous social changes, a growing middle class and an altered public discourse. But importantly it has had its own consequences for the aforementioned local movements with its own internal dynamics. I had also argued the significance of institutionalization which perforce led to a focus on the doable, that what is actually possible in existing conditions. This implies that movements focused on the 'doable'- on policies which did not run counter to the neoliberal development agenda as it unfolded in the 1990s. The compatibility with the neoliberal thinking was a necessary ingredient in the strategy. Much of the programmes on gender and development likewise we saw was compatible with the neoliberal agenda. The new Dalit movement too, it has been argued focused on the 'doable'- on policies which did not run counter to the neoliberal development agenda as it unfolded in the 1990s, on the policies which could be argued from within the neoliberal discourse.

It is important to make the point that neoliberalism appears to be simply set of prescriptions that are practical, that make self-evident sense, innocent of ideologies and politics. But as has been shown it is deeply ideological and like most ideologies has a tendency to be actualized, simply because it is expected to work. In India the ascendancy of neoliberalsim as a vision coincided with the dismantling of an earlier consensus around what goes into the making of the Indian nation and state.

My contention in this paper is to locate the travels of feminism in this swirling melting pot of very diverse sets of ideas and practices. What I would like to argue is that this ideological shift has to be understood in the broader matrix of structural and ideological changes in this late stage of capitalism. The stakes are high. If a demand exists for Dalit capitalism, so does a view that the women's movement is better placed to negotiate with the market rather than the state. That the state is expected to facilitate the process of licenses for Dalit business is part of the story of the constitutive nature of the relationship between the state and market. Understanding nationalism has to take note not just of transnational labour as Hensman does, but the transformation of an earlier era of national capitalist to a transnational capitalist class for quite clearly the role of the bourgeoise whether dalit or indigenous remain pertinent.

What is also discernible in the dominant ideological paradigm in India is that an earlier relative privileging of workers as nation builders is replaced by an almost entirely capitalist or "captains of industry" nation builders. The Finance Minister (FM) and Prime Minister (PM) of India have been routine participants in award ceremonies to captains of industries in recent years. In one the FM made an interesting distinction between what he called an earlier era of organic development of capitalism where Indians built industries and the present stage where they should buy off already established industries in major global take over. NDTV broadcasted live its awards for the Indian of the Year 2008, hosted in Taj Mansingh Hotel on 17th January, 2008 attended by among others industrialists, politicians, the Prime Minister and Finance Minister. The anchor introduced the event mentioning that "India's best and brightest have come together in the room" and that today it is economics, not politics that drive the world. I think both statements emerge as the apparently unproblematic common sense of the neo-liberal era. Indeed politics is seen as disruptive to development. Not surprisingly 'women's empowerment" is viewed as constructive, 'women's unionization and political movements' as obstacles to the furthering of neoliberal policies, now termed "reforms". Yet at this very juncture there are restless claimants to the party. Indeed, Indian nationalism is broader than ever before with more sections engaged with it. Yet at the same time the language of nationalism has changed both because the nature of capital has changed and the social base of capitalists has changed. The globe is the playing field even as the regions and marginalized groups stake claims.

References

Basu, Aparna 1976, "The Role of Women in the Indian Struggle for Freedom" in B.R. Nanda (ed) Indian Women: From Purdah to Modernity (New Delhi, Vikas).

Breman, Jan 2004, "Return of Social Inequality: A Fashionable Doctrine", *Economic and Political Weekly* 39: 35, August 28th, pp. 3869-3872.

Butalia, Urvashi, 2000, *The Other Side of Silence: Voices from the Partition of India* (Duke University Press).

Cambell, John, L. 2004, Institutional Change and Globalisation (Princeton, Princeton University Press).

Chakravarti Uma, 1989, "Whatever happened to the Vedic Dasi? Orientalism, Nationalism and a Script for the Past". Sangari and Sudesh Vaid, *Recasting Women: Essays in Colonial India* (New Delhi, Kali for Women) pp. 27-87.

Chandhoke Neera, 2005, "'Seeing' the State in India", *Economic and Political Weekly* 40:11, March 12th, pp. s1033-1039.

Chaudhuri, Maitrayee, 1993, *The Indian Women's Movement: Reform and Revival* (Delhi, Radiant).

————————1996, "Citizens, Workers and Cultural Emblems: An Analysis of the First Planned Document In India" in Patricia Uberoi (ed), *State, Social Reform and Sexuality*, pp. 211-235. New Delhi: Sage.

————————1998, "Print Media, Advertisements and the New Indian Woman", *Social Action,* July, pp. 239-252.

————————2000, Feminism in Print Media", *Indian Journal of Gender Studies,* September, pp. 263-288.

————————2001, "Gender and Advertisements: The Rhetoric of Globalisation", Women's Studies International Forum Vol. 24 No. 3 / 4, pp. 373-385.

————————2010, *Sociology in India: Intellectual and Institutional Practices* (Jaipur, Rawat).

Dube Muchkund and Jabbi M.K., 2009, *A Social Charter for India: Citizen's Perspective for Basic Rights,* 2009 (Delhi, Pearson Longman).

Geetha, V. 2004, "Periyar, Women and an Ethic of Citizenship" in Maitrayee Chaudhuri (ed) Feminism in India (New Delhi, Kali for Women) pp. 156-174.

Guru Gopal, 2005, "Janus faced Colonialism", *Tarun Udwale,* 20th July.

Hensman Rohini, 2004, "Globalisation, Women and Work: What Are We Talking About?" *Economic and Political Weekly* 39: 10, March 6th, pp.1030-1034.

Illaiha Kancha, 2002, "Cultural Globalization", February 24th, *Outlook. India.com*

John, Mary 1996, "Gender and Development in India, 1970s-1990s: Some reflections on the Constitutive Role of Contexts", *Economic and Political Weekly*, 31 (47): 3071-3077.

——————2009, "Reframing Globalization: Perspectives from the Women's Movement", *Economic and Political Weekly* 44:10, March 7-13, pp.46-50.

Kabeer Naila, 2005, "Women's Empowerment? Analysis of Findings in South Asia", *Economic and Political Weekly* 40:44, pp. 4709-4718.

Kalpagam, U. 1994, *Labour and Gender: Survival in Urban India* (New Delhi, Sage).

Krishnaraj Maithreyi, 2005, "Research in Women Studies: A Need for a Critical Appraisal", *Economic and Political Weekly* 40:28, July 9, pp. 3008 –3017.

Lerche, Jens, 2008, "Transnational Advocacy Networks and Affirmative Action for Dalits in India", *Development and Change* 39(2) 239-261.

Mazumdar Vina, 2001, "Whose Past? Whose History? Whose Tradition? Indigenising Women's Studies in India", *Asian Journal of Women's Studies* (AJWS) 7:1 pp. 133-53.

Menon Ritu and Bhasin, Kamla, 1998, *Borders and Boundaries* (New Jersey, Rutgers University Press).

Omvedt Gail, 2005, "Capitalism and Globalisation, Dalits and Adivasis", *Economic and Political Weekly* 40:47, 19th November pp. 4881-4884.

Patnaik Prabhat, 2005, "Manmohan Singh and Colonialism", *Peoples Democracy,* 17th July.

Phadke Shilpa, 2003, "Thirty Years On: Women's Studies Reflects on the Women's Movement", *Economic and Political Weekly* 38: 43, October 25-31, pp. 4567-4576.

Prasad Chandra Bhan, 2002, "Wealth in the Bhopal Meet", *Pioneer,* January 21st, 2002.

Rege Sharmila, 1998, "Dalit Women talk Differently: A Critique of 'Difference' and Towards a Dalit Feminist Standpoint Position" *Economic and Political Weekly* 33:44, October 31st, WS 39-46.

Roy Anupama, 2005, *Gendered Citizenship: Historical and Conceptual Explorations* (Delhi, Orient Longman).

Roy Kumkum, 1996, "Where women are worshipped, there the gods rejoice: The Mirage of Ancestress of the Hindu Woman", in Tanika Sarkar and Urvashi Butalia (eds.) *Women and the Hindu Right: A Collection of Essays*, (New Delhi, Kali for Women), pp. 181-215.

Sangari Kumkum and Sudesh Vaid, 1989, Recasting Women: Essays in Colonial India (New Delhi, Kali for Women).

Singha Roy Debal K, 2005, "Peasant Movements in Contemporary India: Emerging Forms of Domination and Resistance" *Economic and Political Weekly* 40:52, December 24th, pp. 5505-5515.

Sunder Rajan Rajeshwari, 2003, *The Scandal of the State: Women, Law, and Citizenship* in *Postcolonial India* (Delhi, Permanent Black).

Tenth Five Year Plan 2002-2007 (2003): Governance and Implementation, Vol. 1, Government of India, Planning Commission, Delhi.

Uberoi Patricia, 1996, State, Social Reform and Sexuality, (New Delhi, Sage).

Varma Anuradha, 2009, "It's a corporate take over" *Times Life,* TOI, 19th April, 2009.

Websites and Newspapers:

Countercurrents.org 30 September, 2004.

infochangeindia.org October 15th 2008.

Hindustan Times, Feb1, 2005.

http://www.politicalaffairs.net/article/articleview/1498/

The Times of India (*TOI*), 18th April 2009.

http://timesofindia.indiatimes.com/articleshow/1176547.cms

2

Dalit Women's Movement in Tamil Nadu

Fatima Burnard Nadesan

Five Dalit youth were lynched by a dominant caste Jat community by throwing stones, for carrying a dead cow in village Harithurapura of Jajar district in the state of Haryana on 15th Oct, 2002. The mob stoned them under the presumption that they were skinning a live cow. The misery was that the body of the dead cow was sent for post mortem whereas the bodies of the Dalits were not. This proves the fact that the life of a cow is more valuable and important than the lives of Dalits as claimed by a leader from *Hindu Munnani,* a political wing that promotes Hindutva.

In Tamil Nadu on 12th June, 2002, *Dinakaran*, a Tamil newspaper, reported that at Thinniyam in Trichy District of Tamil Nadu, three Dalits were made to feed each other human excreta, since they raised their voice to get back Rs. 2000, paid as advance for getting houses. The perpetrator had taken money under the false promise of getting house sites for the Dalits. The three Dalits that asked for the money were branded with hot iron rods, beaten up and made to feed each other with human excreta.

Selvi, a poor visually disabled, Dalit girl from Cholankudi Kadu village in Perambalur district of Tamil Nadu, was brutally gang-raped by Vellaiyan, Velmurugan, Elavarasu, Pazhanivel and Sankar. All the perpetrators belong to the Vanniyar caste. Dalits in that village are a numerical minority. The crime was immediately reported to the police who registered the case under Crime No. 5173/2002, of Koovaham police station, under sections 354, 376 and 506(I) of the Indian penal Code and under sections 3(I)(XI), 3(I)(XII) and 3 (2)(V) of the SC/ST (Prevention of Atrocities), Act. The police attested the culprits and they were released on bail. On the same night of their release Elavarasu, Pazhanivel and Sankar set fire to the huts of Selvi and her grand parents. Arsoning of the houses was reported to the police on the next morning.

On 3rd April, 2002, Dalits of Kootharambakkam village in Kanchipuram district under the aegis of Tamil Nadu Dalit Women's Movement (TNDWM) voiced their rights to the share from the common resources and expressed their desire that the chariot of the God in the village temple be brought to their streets. As the streets of the Dalits were considered to be dirty, the chariot of God would never have been taken to their streets. The Dalits were severely beaten up and their houses damaged and the temple festival was celebrated with a police force and did not include the Dalits. TNDWM directly involved in setting right this atrocity represented before the government officials. The officials intervened by constituting a peace committee. In the peace committee meeting it was decided that the Dalits would be given 1/3 share in all the income from all common resources. This was not acceptable to the non-Dalits and they continued to trouble the Dalits in every way.

Where is justice? Where have gone the protections envisaged under various human rights? Who are the Dalits? Where are the protective laws for them?

160 million Dalits live in India facing all kinds of atrocities and discrimination. Dalit is the word given by Dr. Ambedkar which has political identity and which means that Dalits are against the caste system, *Varnashramam*. The word means, "Broken, split and also refer to pollution and Karma theory".

The caste hierarchical system specifies four castes namely the Brahmins (priestly caste), the Kshatriya (warriors), the Vaishyas (traders) and the Shudras (menial task workers). Below this four-tier caste ladder there is another rung of people, who are called the untouchables (Panchamas). Among the untouchables, the status of women is further eroded and closely linked to the concepts of purity and pollution.

B.R. Ambedkar as one of the architects of the Indian constitution was the leader and the foremost guide of the civil rights of the "untouchable" class to which he belonged. His actions and writings have been instrumental in empowering Dalits to ascertain dignity, self-respect, social consciousness, political identity, and the motivation to fight for their basic human rights. He successfully incorporated Article 17 of the Indian Constitution that explicitly declares that untouchability has been abolished. Dr. Ambedkar observed that *Varnashramam* justified untouchability and discriminated Dalits including Dalit Women.

Status of Dalit Women

Dalit women are constantly confronting the hierarchical caste system which perpetuates and maintains the caste hierarchy in order to keep the 160 million people under slavery. Dalit women in the country number nearly 80.5 million. Tamil Nadu has the fifth largest Dalit population in the country, 19.0% of the state population. Within this, Dalit women in Tamil Nadu number 5.9 million, the majority (70.1%) residing in rural areas in the state.[1] 62% of them are illiterate.

Dalit women are landless and mainly work as agricultural labour. Less than 10% of Dalits households have access to drinking water, electricity and toilets. Dalit women are daily victims of the atrocities and face discrimination and unequal treatment. The government also plays role in neglecting the cause of the Dalits and the foremost sufferers are the Dalit women.

The Government of Tamil Nadu had introduced a new ordinance against religious conversion to the infringement of the right of Dalits to free worship. The ordinance curtailed the constitutional safeguards of Dalits and minorities enshrined under Article 25 of the Indian constitution.

The Dalits are treated as outcasts and untouchables since they are not born from the body of Brahma according to *Varnashramam* concepts. They are forced to do ignoble and menial jobs like beating drums at the funerals, clean the villages and towns, sweeping the roads, cleaning toilets and doing manual scavenging, skinning dead animals, shoe making and other kinds of tasks considered degrading for lower wages.

In everyday life, Dalits are humiliated and treated like slaves. They have to work hard for the landlords. Different forms of untouchability are still practised against Dalits in many villages of Tamil Nadu and elsewhere in the country as well. Dalits are served food and water onto their hands, are not allowed to enter the house of landlords, denied entry into temples, not allowed to draw water from common wells, cannot ride a bicycle on the streets of the other castes, are not allowed to enter the streets of other caste wearing shoes and clean dresses, two separate glasses are kept in tea-shops- one for Dalits (glass) and the other one (stainless steel) for other castes and are sometimes served tea in *saratai* which is one half of the coconut shell. Dalit children are made to sit separately in village schools. Drinking water and midday meals in schools are served by other caste, and if a Dalit by accident happens to serve, she or he will be punished. There are even separate washermen and barbers for Dalits in villages, even if they are Dalits themselves. The Dalits and the marginalised are still colonised by the feudal lords and the elites without freedom from caste discrimination. Dalit women are bearing the burden of double day caste and sexual division of labour. Dalit women are demeaned and degraded and their body is a free terrain of colonization by men from other community as well as by Dalits. Dalit women are deprived and are at the lowest strata of the economic, social and educational structures.

A recent report of the *National Commission for Enterprises in the Unorganised Sector* further stated that 87.8% of scheduled castes and scheduled tribes (SC/STs) belong to the poor and vulnerable economic group, forming the highest percentage compared to any other social group.[2] (Dalits are officially addressed as SC). 50% of Dalits still live below the poverty line.

Dalit women are poor, illiterate, sexually harassed, and prone to caste violence, exploitation and subjugated to multiple discrimination. Theirs is a life of daily struggle. They are made to do menial work due to their 'lower' caste status. Although Article 17 of the Indian Constitution declares that untouchability is abolished, in practice it continues to exist in different forms. More than 1.5 million Dalit women in India are engaged in manual scavenging, removing human excreta from the so-called dry toilets in many villages and small towns, an act that lowers their dignity and dehumanizes them. Till today in many villages they are not allowed to take water from the public well and are denied entry in temples.

The food cooked by Dalit women is considered impure as evidenced in the case of Kalyani on 15 July, 2003 in Anaipalayam in Erode District in Tamil Nadu. Kalyani, a Dalit Women assigned to cook nutritious meal in a school faced boycott by the other caste people, who forbade their children from eating the food prepared by her and was dismissed from her job. TNDWM went on a fact-finding mission, after which it mobilised a protest demonstration in front of the district Collectorate. Kalyani was reinstated at the same job in the same school.

Dalit women face systematic violence in community. Every hour two Dalits are assaulted. Everyday three Dalit Women are raped, two Dalits are murdered and two Dalit houses are burnt in India. Dalit women are raped at work place and in their homes by both the State (police) and by Non-State actors (upper caste men). Such violence against Dalit women becomes possible because of the culture of purity and pollution that isolates them.

The issue of Dalit women deserves attention of the Human Rights Council in relevant thematic debates and country reviews. In her report to the 11th session of the Human Rights Council, the Special Rapporteur on violence against women, its causes and consequences, Ms. Yakin Ertürk, addressed a number of cases of violence against Dalit women. The serious forms of discrimination, sexual exploitation, and violence that Dalit women are often subjected to may also serve as an illustrative example of the impediments to equality before the law. Violence against Dalit women presents clear evidence of widespread exploitation and discrimination against these women, who are subordinated in terms of power relations to men in a patriarchal and caste-dominant society. This report was submitted to the 70th Session of the Committee on the Elimination of Race Discrimination in Geneva, Switzerland in January 2007. Demeaning social customs include the *Devadasi* system (temple dancer-prostitutes) throughout Tamil Nadu, the system of "*mathamma*" or forced prostitution in North Arcot district of Tamil Nadu, and the practice of manual scavenging were mentioned in the report. The observations were based on the evidence provided by the Dalit Women's Movement and the report submitted by Tamil Nadu Women's Forum.

During the High Commissioner's visit to Nepal and India in March 2009, Ms. Pillay, the High Commissioner of UNHRC (United Nations Human Rights Commission) urged the respective governments to effectively address the issue of caste-based discrimination, both as a national and an international human rights problem. This is the strongest support ever shown by the principal human rights official of the UN to the global fight against caste-based discrimination, which was reaffirmed during the Durban Review Conference where she said that "she personally felt that "related intolerance" [in the DDPA-Durban Declaration and Plan of Action] would cover discrimination on the basis of caste, class and social status."

Dalit women are sexually exploited and violence against Dalit women are legitimized. Due to social exclusion Dalit women are kept voiceless, raped and killed. The number of persons affected in caste atrocities, approximately 260 million people worldwide, and the range and severity of human rights violations indicate that this is one of the biggest, yet most overlooked human rights problems that face the affected countries and the international community today. (HRC 11 Statement-item 2).

Dalit women are thrice discriminated, treated as untouchables and as outcasts, due to lower caste strata. Face gender discrimination for being women, and finally economic impoverishment due to deprivation of access to productive resources, unequal wages, with low or underpaid labour system. The caste discrimination inherited by birth leaves Dalit women facing multiple oppressions and subjugates them to various forms of discrimination. These women are the poorest, illiterate and easy targets for sexual harassment. They face not just caste violence inflicted on them by the dominant castes, but also state violence. The forms of state violence include custodial torture, custodial rape, destruction of property and belongings by the police, brutal beating causing mutilation of genitals, outraging modesty and abdominal kicks aiming at harming uterus and causing miscarriages. The law enforcers do not file cases on the complaints given by the dalits.

The cruel custodial rapes of Rajammal and Murugammal by the Ramnad police in Tamil Nadu that took place on 11 October 2002, are very common. The police excesses on the Dalit women of Manjolai, Gundupatti, Ogalore and Polanayakkapalayam villages bear testimony on state-perpetrated violence. Whenever the Dalit women have demanded justice either for arbitrary arrest or for custodial harassment they were lathi-charged and attacked by police. In the case of the tea estate workers of Manjolai who were seeking a wage hike on 23 July 1999, 17 Dalit women were caused to drown in the Tamirabarani river along with their children.

The UN Special Rapporteur on Violence against Women has noted that "[Dalit women] face targeted violence, even rape and death from state actors and powerful members of dominant castes, used to inflict political lessons and crush dissent within the community.[3]

Across India, of the 25,880 crimes against SCs where police completed investigation in 2005, 85.9% of cases saw police submitting the cases for trial. In Tamil Nadu in the same year, 73.5% of cases saw police submit a Final Report True or charge sheet cases for trial.[4] However, of the 20,640 cases of crimes against SCs across the country (a mere 18.9% of cases for trial) for which trials were completed that year, only 29.8% ended in convictions.

Dalit women are poor and landless and they work round the clock for their survival. In 2004-05, only 38% of Dalits in India owned any land. *Panjami* land which was given to Dalits by the British Government are now encroached by other communities. There are 12.5 lakhs acres of *Panjami* land, out of which Dalits enjoy only 0.025% of lands. The significance of low levels of land ownership combined with poverty is that the majority of Dalit women eke out their livelihood by engaging in waged labour occupations in the unorganised sector. At the same time, their contribution as a significant workforce in the national economy is revealed through their higher work participation rate (29.4% all-India, 40.3% in Tamil Nadu) than women in general (25.7% all-India, 31.5% in Tamil Nadu).

Moreover, the overwhelming majority of Scheduled Caste women main and marginal (working for less than six months per year) workers are concentrated in the unorganised sector in rural areas as agricultural labourers (57.4% all-India, 69.4% in Tamil Nadu), with less than 10% cultivating land (18.1% all-India, 9.1% in Tamil Nadu). A further small percent are household industry workers (5.6% all-India, 3.5% in Tamil Nadu), while the remaining are engaged in other occupations (19% all-India, 18.1% in Tamil Nadu).

The right to primary education has been declared a fundamental right under the newly inserted Article 21A of the Indian Constitution. In spite of the same in Tamil Nadu, only 53% of Dalit women are literate. The school dropout rates among Dalit girls remain high, with 74.2% of Dalit girls in India dropping out between 1st to 10th standards, as compared to 63.9% for girls in general.[5] In Tamil Nadu, the dropout rate for Dalit girls between 1st to 10th standards is 46.3%.[6] The formal education schemes are still not reaching out to Dalit girls.

Dalit women are deprived of political space. They remain only as voters. They have to vote for a candidate as forced by the dominant caste leaders. Women's reservation in local governments gives an opportunity, but this opportunity is also denied to them by men from the same caste and from the dominant caste. Any refusal or assertion will end up either in brutal murder as witnessed in the case of Meneka on 15th July 2004, or dismissal from office as evidenced in the case of Ranganayagi. There are 285 Dalit women officially elected in the Panchayat.

At the level of India's Panchayati Raj or decentralised local governance system, the *73rd Constitutional Amendment Act, 1992* reserves seats for scheduled castes in proportion to their population in the state, and 33% of Panchayat seats for women. Within the scheduled caste (Dalit) category, one-third of all seats are reserved for scheduled caste women. However, reservations run up against huge hurdles in implementation, particularly dominant caste interests in preventing Dalits from accessing political power and resources for development. Recent research has revealed that in many SC Women reserved panchayats, political power often still remained with the dominant caste members, effectively preventing Dalit women elected representatives from voicing their development concerns in panchayat meetings and influencing the allocation of development benefits for their communities.[7]

Ranganayaki the elected president of the village Panchayat (the local self governance body in the three tier governance system in India) solemnized an inter-caste wedding of Vijayarangan, S/o Subramani, who belonged to the Vanniyar caste and Gowri, D/o.Ponnan, who hails from the Dalit Community. This became the source of discrimination against Ranganayaki and caste enmity by other caste members of the local body. The Non-Dalit members of the local body made various false allegations to the Collector and Panchayat union authority against the President and ultimately disrupted her functioning. Due to the petition an inquiry was held and following that, she was removed from the post of President.

In Tamil Nadu, caste tensions during the 2001 elections resulted in 96 SC reserved seats lying vacant, over half being for Dalit women.[8] Subsequent by-elections to fill vacant reserved seats often encountered caste resistance. As per the *Concluding Observations* of the CERD Committee on the Indian Government's Report in 2007, *"Dalit candidates, especially women, are frequently forcibly prevented from standing for election or, if elected, forced to resign from village councils or other elected bodies or not to exercise their mandate."*[9]

Dalit women perform dance which is devoted to *Mathamma* the clan goddess goddess(*Kulathaivam*) of the community of Dalit *Arunthatiyar*. The dancer is, however, almost exploited as being expected to dance in an erotic way. The month of June (*Aani* in Tamil Calendar) is the temple festival for five days, when the *Mathamma* temple is built, and the festival conducted, by the other castes. After the 5th day of the festival, Dalit girl children who are sick, are dedicated to the goddess believing that those children will be cured by the healing power of goddess, *Mathamma*. Once the child is cured, she is married to the goddess and is named after the goddess *Mathamma*. She becomes a powerful replica of *Mathamma*. Later on she is mocked and treated as a public property. She is denied and deprived of the right to a normal life and cannot marry; however the men from other castes and from her own community use her. The children born out of such relationship face humiliation in society and even in school in case they happen to get enrolled. *Mathammas* are socially and economically exploited by the community. They have to live on their own without the support of their families. *Mathamma* being a Dalit woman, becomes a dancer, then sexually exploited and ends up with nothing but diseases.

This dominant brutal culture which originated from the *Devadasi* system is extended to the Dalit community and is still prevailing among Dalit women. Instigated by the dominant religious forces, the Dalit men harassed the Tamil Nadu Dalit Women's Movement (TNDWM) for exposing the issue of *Mathamma*. Dalit women who were dedicated to *Mathamma* have joined the *Mathamma* movement which began in 2000. They go from village to village explaining to their own communities the pain and agony they have faced for being a *Mathamma*. They have succeeded in stopping the practice in 3 districts of Vellore, Thiruvellore and in Kancheepuram. They have been named as *Mathamma* and every one called them as *Mathamma*. Due to this they have changed their names and their identity and called themselves like other Dalit women as Devi, Renuka etc.

Their Present Economic Situation

At present, 1,34,000 hectares of lands are earmarked for 67 multi-product SEZs (Special Economic Zones) in India (*Financial Express*, 30 Aug. 2006). Although the landowner might receive the compensation for the land acquired for SEZs, the peasant Dalit women are facing the peril of the livelihoods by losing their job as well as being evicted from the land.

For Dalit women, "trickle-down effect" theory, in which people can expect "trickled" benefits dropped down from the country or the economic growth of big companies, is just a mirage, not a reality at all.

The state of Tamil Nadu behaves as an agent of the Multi National Corporation (MNCs). The state government which is essentially responsible for the welfare of the citizens not only becomes advocates of the corporations but also acts as a corporation. The state government takes away the land, especially agricultural lands, coastal lands, salt pans, and forest lands for SEZs. Only 35% of the acquired land taken for SEZs is used for industry and the rest for non-industrial purposes such as recreation centres and housing. Although people are resisting by raising their voice, the oppression from the state government is intensified.

There were vociferous protests against the proposal of Tata's titanium dioxide plant to be established, at Sathankulam of Tuticorin district, in Tamil Nadu, in 2007. The ruling party was very adamant and urged the panchayat leaders to accept the project. The state government further went ahead and made an agreement with the company for establishing the Rs 2,500-crore titanium dioxide project even before the Panchayat leaders had complied with the formalities of submitting their acceptance for the project. Negligence of local people voices in the politics, and economy in SEZs definitely erodes the livelihood of the most vulnerable groups in the region, the Dalit Women.

They affect peasant landless Dalit women by displacing them from the lands without any compensation. The SEZs only employ poor Dalit women as manual labourers. When returning from the factory to their homes late at night, they have no safety. In Ulundurpettai taluk of Villupuram district in Tamil Nadu on 7 March, 2007 there were 3 rapes – one was a Dalit woman, and the other women were from other communities. All of them were workers in big factories, and attacked on their way home from their workplace.

Floriculture

A study by the Tamil Nadu Women's Forum on the impact of floriculture on the health of Dalit women disclosed that in Santana Gopalapuram in Tamil Nadu, floriculture has rapidly increased in the last 5 years, thereby displacing farmers from agriculture. The crops grown earlier such as groundnut and rice are now found very sporadically. The Dalit women had to work on the farm from 6 in the morning. They suffered chest and back pains, due to constant bending and plucking of flowers for almost 6 hours at a stretch for low wages. They further suffered from spraying of pesticides.

Women suffered from excessive white discharges, rolling feeling in the stomach, hysterectomy, and tumour in uterus.

In Kollathur a Dalit village in Tamil Nadu, the agricultural lands were taken away for aqua-farm for prawn export. Dalits were occupied as cultivators of cashewnuts and fishers of shrimps and fishes in the backwater. In 2004, an aqua-farm came up on their agricultural land, right alongside the backwaters. The aqua-farm discharged untreated effluents from the farm which salinated agricultural lands and the backwaters and took away livelihood resources of Dalit women. This was in violation of the verdict of the Indian Supreme Court that pronounced a judgement for regulating the use of coastal area for environmental protection.

The toxic waste from the aqua-farm causes loss of agricultural production which affects directly the daily food production of the Dalit villagers. This causes food insecurity as well as livelihood insecurity to Dalit women. The toxic waste has polluted human beings, mostly Dalit women who work in the fields directly. Women got itching, skin disease and dimming of eyesight. Ground water has been salinated, and Dalit women lost adequate water for agriculture as well as for drinking.

Tamil Nadu Dalit Women's Movement (TNDWM)

TNDWM promoted in the year 1997 has been voicing for the rights of Dalit women. In fact, the movement emerged as a response during the process of addressing the caste atrocities on Dalit women at Rasapalayam area in the state of Tamil Nadu. Restoring lands taken away and registering them in the name of

Dalit women has been the prime focus of TNDWM. Ensuring equal living wage to Dalit women, equal share of common property resources, preventing displacement from lands, eradicating the practice of manual scavenging and *jogini* system are the few core areas of intervention.

TNDWM voices for the rights of Dalit women at various levels from local to international level and has made visible inroads into other movements, political parties, bureaucrats, media, and continue the struggle against caste oppression, communalism and fundamentalism. Whenever atrocities occurred, the movement is instrumental in taking up Dalit issues at various national and international forums. In the year 2000, TNDWM leaders were trained in Sri Lanka by Asia Pacific Forum on Law and Development (APWLD) on how to lobby during World Conference Against Racism (WCAR) in Durban. In 2001, leaders participated in the conference in Durban. Dalit activists formed a cultural troop called *Viduthalai kalai kuzu* and went around Denmark in 2003 with the programme called 'Images of Asia'. In support of the farmers and joining the people's movement, Dalit women leaders joined the protest against the 6th Ministrial meeting of WTO in Hongkong. Exposing the caste discrimination and the atrocities on Dalit women, the leaders of TNDWM went around Asian countries and attended international forums in Indonesia, Philippines, Bangkok, Malaysia, Japan, Bangladesh, Korea, China and Cambodia exposing caste discrimination and the atrocities on Dalit women. They went to 16 Asian countries to support the issue of Food Sovereignty, Campaigning against GMO (Genetically Modified Organisms), and Globalization.

In March 2004, a 3 year old Dalit girl from Chinnammapettai was brutally raped by a 16 year old boy. Though the matter was reported to the police they failed to take action. The parent approached Tamil Nadu Dalit Women's Movement. Tamil Nadu Dalit Women's Movement undertook a fact finding trip and based on the report a public meeting was organized. The public meeting demanded stringent punishment for the perpetrator and insisted that the state adhere to preventive measures against such practices.

In Pazhaiyanur village of Sivaganga District, a Dalit women Lakshmi aged 18 years was sexually assaulted by Bhakyaraj, another caste man, when she was on her way to her work. The police failed to register a case against the culprit. He threatened to kill her and the parents in case of her complaining to the police. The TNDWM took up the issue before the appropriate forums and succeeded to register a case against the culprit.

Kattuparamagudi is a village in Sivaganga District, Tamil Nadu where 15 Dalit families are living. Karupi is one of the Dalit women there. She was working as a housemaid in the house of Prema, a teacher in the school of the same village. Prema belongs to the Kallar community. On 26th November 2003, Karupi was arrested by the police of Paramagudi police station on the basis of case filed by Ms. Prema regarding robbery of jewellery in her house. On 1st December 2003, a fisherman noticed that a women's body, the body of Karupi, was hanging from the telephone tower of the police station. Immediately TNDWM visited the village and interacted with the survivors and few members from the perpetrator's community. TNDWM along with local

Dalit Movements organised a joint action of protest and demonstration at Paramagudi.

Muthumari (38), a Dalit woman of Keezha Urappanur village in Madurai district was molested by another caste man Raja (40). He had been attempting to subject her to sexual assault over the past six months. She protested and reported the same to her house. He took the issue to the village elders. The next day, a group of persons including Raja, his wife, Vijaya and their relatives came there and hurled abuses at Muthumari, pulled her by the sari and hit her in the chest and abdomen and splashed human excreta-mixed water on her face and chest. For fear of life she did not lodge any complaint. TNDWM intervened and took the case before the police. However, the movement had to face a stiff challenge for taking the issue ahead.

Dalit women through the movement are taking up political issues and strengthening the movement with strong leaderships. Dalit women demand Right to freedom for dignity and choice, Right to development and participation. Protection and promotion of Dalit women's land and political rights are the key focus area of TNDWM. Using the space the TNDWM has facilitated Dalit women to participate in the political spaces by contesting as candidates, by effective use of their right to franchise and participating in the democratic forums.

TNDWM supports Dalit children to continue education such as teacher training, catering, and nursing. The movement assisted children to get health support for open heart surgery and for orthopaedic care.

At Ramakrishnapuram, the movement agitated for a graveyard and succeeded in getting the place and also pathway to the cremation ground. In 2005 at Thazavedu, the *Arunthathier* community was denied water supply by the other community. After the intervention by the Movement the supply was resumed.

TNDWM supported *Mathammas* to challenge the discriminative practices for economic enhancement through economic support programs. They ensured that no more children were dedicated to the dirty.

The support of the Tamil Nadu Dalit Women's Movement for political participation of Dalit women motivated the *Mathammas*, sex workers and other Dalit women leaders to contest as candidates in the democratic electoral process. Two Mathammas, Devi and Renuka, motivated by the movement came out from the practice and in spite of all opposition from their own community contested in the state assembly elections.

During the Fifteenth general election to the Indian parliament in the year 2009, Ms. Rajamani aged 52, a Dalit women district leader of TNDWM along with seven other district leaders contested from Vellore in Tamil Nadu. These Dalit women are poor and had no educational background. When Ms. Rajamani went to the Collector's office to file the nomination form, she was the only woman among the wealthy politicians who teased her. She pledged her jewels for paying the deposit. Sensing her popularity the political parties approached her to contest under their banner. She refused and contested in the name of TNDWM, as an independent candidate under the symbol of a Sewing machine. The movement members extended their support and mobilized the people to collect funds to meet the expenses. She secured 4138 votes and the same was a big achievement taking into account the fact that she contested against the very powerful ruling party and the wealthy giants.

The election proved that the movement has strong footing in the state and is capable of negotiating with the mighty political wizards. This was an opportunity for the TNDWM to extend their efforts at lower levels.

TNDWM continues to face harassment for confronting the caste and patriarchal norms of the communities which is influenced by Hindutva ideology that perpetuates hatred towards other religion and maintains the culture that is exploitative and brutally dominant. TNDWM believes that caste is the enemy of humanity and if it is not killed, caste will kill the Dalits.

At present in Tamil Nadu there are fifteen Women's Movements which have been led by Dalit women. These are given below:

Table 1 : Dalit Women's Movements in Tamil Nadu

No.	*Movement Name*	*District*	*Person Name*
1.	Arunthathiyar Women's Movement	Sivagasi	Perumal Ammal
2.	Swathi Women's Movement	Karur	Christy
3.	Arunthathiyar Women's Forum	Nellai	Muthumariyammal
4.	Arul Oli Movement	Chennai	Jeyalakshi
5.	Rural Women Development Trust	Salem	Alamelu
6.	Ulupavarkay Nilam Sontham	Thanjavur	Krishnammal
7.	Athi Tamilar Peravai pengal Amaipu	Coimbatore	Deepa

(Contd.)

(Contd. Table 1)

No.	Movement Name	District	Person Name
8.	Dalit Women's Movement	Sivagangai	Maythinam
9.	Lead Trust	Madurai	Jeya
10.	AIDWA Dalit Women	Virudunager	Suganthi
11.	Dalit women's Liberation Movement	Sivagangai	Vironika
12.	Thental Movement	Thiruvannamalai	Veda
13.	Sangam Women's Movement	Pondichery	Veerammal
14.	Women's Collective	Nellai	Ponnuthai
15.	Dalit Women's Movement	Thiruvannamalai	Rajammal

India has celebrated 62 years of Independence. The country is now recording economic growth every year and successfully plays an important and dominant role in international politics and in the economic arena. The success of India is built up on the international reputation of well-educated human resources, "democratic and stable" political circumstances, and promises of land, benefits and other resources to the foreign and national investors. On the other side of this glossy picture there is suffering and misery at the expense and exploitation of Dalit women. In reality India remains the world leader in maternal mortality, female infanticide and foeticide, deaths due to preventive diseases, and other indicators of poor human development and a society which is highly hierarchical and caste dominated.

Notes

1. Government of India, *Census of India 2001: Primary Census Abstract* (New Delhi: Government of India, 2001).

2. National Commission for Enterprises in the Unorganised Sector, *Report on the Conditions of Work and Promotion of Livelihoods in the Unorganised Sector* (New Delhi: NCEUS, 2007).
3. UN Special Rapporteur on Violence against Women, 2002. *Cultural Practices in the Family that are Violent towards Women,* UN Doc. E/CN.4/2002/83, para.53.
4. National Crimes Records Bureau, *Crimes in India 2005 Report* (New Delhi: NCRB, 2006), Tables 7.3, 7.4.
5. Ministry of Human Resource Development, *Annual Report 2006-2007, Annexure: Selected Educational Statistics 2004-05 (provisional),* (New Delhi: Ministry of Human Resource Development, 2007).
6. Ministry of Human Resource Development, *Selected Educational Statistics 2002-03* (New Delhi: Ministry of Human Resource Development, 2003).
7. Mangubhai J., Irudayam A. and Sydenham E., *Dalit Women's Right to Political Participation in Rural Panchayati Raj: A study of Gujarat and Tamil Nadu* (Madurai: Justitia et Pax, IDEAS and Equalinrights, 2009).
8. Tamil Nadu State Election Commission, *2001 Panchayati Raj Election Results* (2001).
9. UN Doc. CERD/C/IND/CO/19.

References

Agarwal, S. 1999, "Genocide of women in Hinduism", Sudrastan Books, Jabalpur. Online: http://www.geocities.com/realitywithbite/hindu.htm retrieved on 8th Sept, 2007.

Burnad, Fatima N. 2007, 'Land, Livelihood and Access to Resources', paper presented at *Rural Women's Regional Consultation 2007*, Manila, Philippines.

Jalindar, Adsule 2007, 'Globalisation: Dalits at the Crossroads', *The Movement of India*, Vol. II, Issue. 3, pp. 7-8, and 20.

Jayaraman, Nityanand 2007, 'Against All Odds: A Dalit village's fight against industrial aquaculture', *Speak Out!* Vol. June 2007, PCFS/PANAP, Penang.

Kumar, Vinoj P.C. 2007, 'Karunanidhi's Nandigram', Tehelka, 18 Aug 2007.

Moses, Seenarine 1996, 'Dalit Women: Victims or beneficiaries of Affirmative Action Policies in India – A Case Study', *paper presented at a Brown Bag Lecture held by the Southern Asian Institute*, Columbia University, on April. 10th, 1996.

Moses, Seenarine 1996, 'Education of Dalit Women', a paper presented on Saxakali.com.

Muthumary, J 2000, 'Dalit women in India', paper prepared for *International Conference on Dalit Human Rights* 16-17 September, 2000, Shri Guru Ravidass Community Centre at 28 Carlyle Road, Manor Park, London.

Prasad, Chandra Bhan 2004, *Dalit Diary: 1999-2003- Reflections on Apartheid in India*, Navayana Publishing, Pondicherry.

Rajagopal, Balakrishnan 2007, 'The caste system — India's apartheid?' The Hindu.

Thind, G. S. 2000, "Our Indian Sub-Continent Heritage" Crosstown Press, British Columbia.

3

Gender Audit of Budgets in India (2001-2 to 2009-10)

Vibhuti Patel

Introduction

This chapter attempts a gender audit of budgets in India in the recent years. Budget is an important tool in the hands of state for affirmative action for improvement of gender relations through reduction of gender gap in the development process. It can help to reduce economic inequalities, between men and women as well as between the rich and the poor. Hence the budgetary policies need to keep into considerations the gender dynamics operating in the economy and in the civil society. There is a need to stress the importance of participatory approaches, bottom up budget, child budget, green budgeting, local and global implications of pro-poor and pro-women budgeting, and inter-linkages between gender-sensitive budgeting and women's empowerment.

Understanding the relationship between macro economic policies and the Union Budget, state budgets and the local self government institutions in the context of economic reforms and globalisation is a MUST as it has influenced women's lives in several ways. It is good economic sense to make national budgets gender-sensitive, as this will enable more effective targeting of government expenditure to women specific activities and reduce inequitable consequences of previous fiscal policies. The Gender Budget Initiative is a policy framework, methodology and set of tools to assist governments to integrate a gender perspective into the budget as the main national plan of public expenditure. It also aims to facilitate attention to gender analysis in review of macro-economic performance, ministerial budget preparations, parliamentary debate and mainstream media coverage. Budget impacts women's lives in several ways. It directly promotes women's development through allocation of budgetary funds for women's programmes, or reduces opportunities for empowerment of women through budgetary cuts.

Gender budgeting is gaining increasing acceptance as a tool for engendering macro-economic policy-making. The Fourth World Conference of Women held in Beijing in September 1995 and the Platform for Action that it adopted, called for a gender perspective in all macro-economic policies and their budgetary dimensions. The Outcome Document of the UN General Assembly Special Session on Women held in June 2000, also called upon all the nations to mainstream a gender perspective into key macro-economic and social development policies and national development programmes. Emphasis on gender budgeting was also placed by the Sixth Conference of Commonwealth Ministers of Women's Affairs held in New Delhi in April 2000.

In India, till 2004, the process of gender budgeting was a post-facto effort to dissect/ analyse and thus offset any undesirable gender-specific consequences of the previous budget. But 2005 onwards, the scenario has changed. Due to consistent lobbying by the gender economists and women's groups; for the first time, in 2005, the Ministry of Finance gave a mandate to all ministries to establish a Gender Budgeting Cell by January, 2005. At present, 54 ministries and departments have formed gender budget cells and have provided annual reports and performance budgets highlighting budgetary allocations for women. The first Gender Budgeting Statement (GBS) in the Union Budget 2005-06 included 10 demands of grants. In 2006-07, the GBS got expanded to 24 demands for grants under 18 ministries/ departments of the Union government and 5 Union Territories. During the current financial year, i.e., 2009-10, the GB Statements covered 34 demands for grants under 27 ministries/ departments and 5 Union Territories.

Macro Economic Scenario

Structural adjustment programmes and globalisation policies have directly increased women's unpaid work burden, thereby increased women-provided subsidy in the economy (Patel, 2009). Devaluation of real income due to inflation leading to price rise of essential commodities and services, erosion of public distribution system and reduction of services offered by the public health system, trafficking of girls for child-labour, sex trade and forced marriage as a result of destitution, privatization of education and the rising male unemployment in traditional sectors have made women bear disproportionate share of burden. In the patriarchal families, women have to shoulder responsibility of providing meals and looking after the sick family members. Women have high stakes in preventing an increase in the proportion of indirect taxes on essential commodities and in budgetary provisions to guarantee food security, good quality of education and health care. Hence, careful study of the working of PDS and local taxonomy on food security and impact on nutrition, education, employment generation, health and health services of budgetary allocations is a must (Patel, 2002).

Implications of the Planning Process on Gender Budget

The planning Commission of India has always focused on women's issues as per the perceptions of their members on women's status within the economy.

The First Five Year Plan (1951-1956) set up Central Social Welfare Board in 1953 to promote welfare work through voluntary organisations, charitable trusts and philanthropic agencies.

The Second Five Year Plan (1956-1960) supported development of Mahila mandals for grass roots work among women.

The Third, Fourth and Interim Plans (1961-74) made provision for women's education, pre-natal and child health services, supplementary feeding for children, nursing and expectant mothers.

The Fifth Plan (1974-1978) marked a major shift in the approach towards women, from 'welfare' to 'development', labeled by the women's studies scholar as WID (Women in Development approach).

The Sixth Plan (1980-85) accepted women's development as a separate economic agenda. The Multidisciplinary approach with three-pronged thrust on health, education and employment was introduced. From the Sixth Five Year Plan onwards, the plan document has been including a separate chapter on women and children.

The Seventh Plan (1985-1990) declared as its objective to bring women into the mainstream of national development. During this period, the Department of women and child development was established within the Ministry of Human Resource Development (MHRD) of the Government of India (GoI). The Seventh Plan introduced the concept of monitoring of 27 beneficiary oriented schemes for women by DWCD. The exercise continues and number of schemes covered is being expanded. The women's studies scholars consider it a WAD (Women And Development) approach.

The Eighth Plan (1992-1997) projected paradigm shift, from development to empowerment and promised to ensure flow of benefits to women in the core sectors of education, health and employment. Outlay for women rose from 4 crores in the First plan to Rs. 2000 crores in the 8th Plan. The Eighth Plan highlighted for the first time, a gender perspective and the need to ensure a definite flow of funds from the general developmental sectors to women. The Plan document made an explicit statement that "....the benefits to development from different sectors should not by pass women and special programmes on women should complement the general development programmes. The latter, in turn, should reflect great gender sensitivity". With this plan GAD (Gender and Development) approach became popular among the policy makers.

The Ninth Plan (1997-2002) stated that empowerment of women was its strategic objective and adopted 'Women Component Plan' (WCP) as one of the major strategies and directed both the Central and State Governments to ensure "not less than 30 per cent of the funds/benefits are earmarked in all the women-related sectors." Special vigil was advocated on the flow of the earmarked funds/benefits through an effective mechanism to ensure that the proposed strategy brings forth a holistic approach towards empowering women. The National Policy for Empowerment of Women, 2001 of GOI adopted during this period envisaged introduction of a gender perspective in the budgeting process as an operational strategy.

Regarding formulation of Gender Development Indices, National Policy for Empowerment of Women, 2001 stated, "In order to support better planning and programme formulation and adequate allocation of resources, Gender Development Indices (GDI) will be developed by networking with specialized agencies. Gender auditing and development of evaluation mechanisms will also be undertaken alongside. Collection of gender disaggregated data by all primary data collecting agencies of the Central and State Governments as well as research and academic institutions in the Public and Private Sectors will be undertaken. Data and information gaps in vital areas reflecting the status of women will be sought to be filled in. All Ministries, Corporations, Banks and financial institutions, etc., will be advised to collect, collate, disseminate data related to programmes and benefits on a gender-disaggregated basis. This will help in meaningful planning and evaluation of policies."

The Tenth Five Year Plan (2002-2007) suggested specific strategies, policies and programmes for empowerment of women. It appreciated efforts at ensuring gender-just and gender-sensitive budget and promised to continue the process of dissecting the government budget to establish its gender-differential impact and to translate gender commitment to budgetary commitments. It made provision of outlay of Rs. 13,780 crores. It accepted that Women Component Plan and Gender Budget play complimentary role for effective convergence, proper utilisation and monitoring of fund from various developmental sectors. The Ministry of Women and Child Development was established during this plan period.

The Eleventh Five Year Plan (2007-2012) demands gender mainstreaming and mentions "Gender Equity requires adequate provisions to be made in policies and schemes across Ministries and Departments. It also entails 'strict adherence to gender budgeting across the board'. It promises special focussed efforts for creation of 'an enabling environment for women to become economically, politically and socially empowered'.

Gender Audit of Union Budgets

Women's status and women's bargaining power in the economy have a major bearing in the budgetary allocations. "Gender Budgeting consists of empirical exercises that focus on public policies and aim to bring out their gender specific implications" (Banerjee, 2002) Yearly analysis of the budget from the point of view of women is a must to enhance women's economic interest and socio-political standing in the economy. Analysis of budget from gender perspective makes us understand what are the nature, character and content of women's share of the development cake. Women's groups and gender economists started dissecting union budgets with gender concerns from 2001 onwards. The year 2001 was declared as 'Women Empowerment Year' by the government.

The gender budgeting initiative in India started in July 2000 when a Workshop on 'Engendering National Budgets in the South Asia Region' was held in New Delhi in collaboration with the UNIFEM, in which Government representatives, UN agencies, media, NGOs, research institutions, civil society and members of the Planning Commission in the South Asia region participated. Noted gender auditing professional Professor Diane Elson made a presentation and shared her experiences on gender budgeting through an interactive session. National Institute of Public Finance and Policy (NIPF&P) was commissioned to study Gender Related Economic Policy Issues, which included gender segregation of relevant macro data, quantification of contribution of women in economy, assessment of impact of Government Budget on women, the role women can play in improving institutional framework for delivery of public services and the policy alternatives for building a gender sensitive national budgeting process.

Certain public expenditure schemes have pro-women allocations, though they are not exclusively targeted for women, for instance, Swarna Jayanti Swarozgar Yojana, Integrated Child Development Scheme, National Education Programme, Sarva Shiksha Abhiyan, District Primary Education Programme (DPEP) etc.

The gender disaggregated public incidence analysis of elementary education budget reveals that girls received around 40 per cent of total public spending on elementary education. On a per capita basis, share of girls worked out at Rs. 286 against Rs. 344 per boy at elementary school stage.

The study concluded that gender incidence of the benefits of public expenditure is difficult to measure in precise quantitative terms, since the bulk of the expenditures are meant to provide services that are essentially public in nature. For instance, all citizens irrespective of caste, creed or sex enjoy the benefits of expenditures on defense, maintenance of law and order and dispensation of justice. Nevertheless, considering the gender bias inherent in a male dominated society the budget should provide some idea about how much is earmarked specifically for the benefit of women. The suggestion is not that the gender-wise break-up of all government expenditures should be provided but that the expenditures meant primarily for women be shown separately so that they can be easily culled out from budget heads of social and economic services in which it is possible to segregate such expenditures. Efforts of gender economists were targeted to evolve mechanism to collate gender disaggregated data from relevant Departments be developed to obtain the gender-wise relevant statistical database, targets and indicators; provide gender audit of plans, policies and programmes of various Ministries with pro-women allocations and lobby for segregated provisions for women in the composite programmes under education, health, employment, housing and rural development, etc. to protect the provisions by placing restrictions on their re-appropriation for other purposes.

Discourse on Gender Budgeting in India during the last Decade

During the last one decade the discourse on Gender Budgeting has revolved around the following issues:

Child Sex Ratio: The Census of India, 2001 revealed further decline in the child sex ratio in several parts of India. In the urban centers, deficit of girls has been enhancing due to pre-birth elimination. In spite of demand of women's groups and recommendation of the Eleventh Five Year Plan to revisit the two child norm laws, several state governments continue to victimize the victim, namely poor, dalit, tribal and Muslim women and unborn girls (as the norm has resulted into intensified sex selective abortions). More budgetary allocation was demanded to implement Pre-conception and Pre-natal Diagnostic Test Act (2002) to prevent sex selective abortion of female fetuses.

Reproductive and Child Health: Evaluation of Chiranjivi Scheme to halt maternal mortality has revealed that the public private partnership in this scheme allows private practitioners to make gains of tax payers money without giving necessary relief to pregnant women. Only in cases of normal delivery, the private practitioner admit women for delivery and in case of complicated delivery, the concerned women are sent to over-crowded public hospital. In National Rural Health Mission (NRHM), the woman health workers are not paid even minimum wages and are paid "honorarium". More budgetary allocation is demanded to ensure statutory minimum wages to them.

Integrated Child Development Scheme (ICDS): Restructuring of ICDS must promote convergence of several schemes of different ministries such as health, rural development, tribal development, JNNURM targeting children. Though the Eleventh Five Year Plan (2007-2012) promised 'Walk-in ICDS centers' at railway stations and bus stands for migrant women and children, none has started yet; not even in the megapolis such as Mumbai, Delhi, Kolkata and Chennai!

Under category of 100% allocation for women, institutional support for women survivors of violence need major attention, but so far not much has been done regarding Scheme for Relief and Rehabilitation of Victims of Sexual Assault promised by the Five Year Plans since 2000. Women's groups providing support to women survivors of Domestic violence are highly disappointed as no separate allocation for Implementation of Domestic Violence Act, 2005 which had defined major role of service providers such as hospitals, law and order machinery, protection office/ counsellor and shelter homes.

Budgetary Allocation for Water Supply and Sanitation that affects women's life greatly as consumers and unpaid and partially paid-workers, does not mention women. This will perpetuate 'unproductive female workload of fetching water from long distance' avers Indira Rajaram (2007). She demands, "water-sheds in the country need to be contoured on the Geographical Information systems (GIS) platform. Using space technology for mapping of acquifiers, a five year plan needs to be drawn up for creating sustainable water sources within reasonable reach of rural habitation." (Rajaram, 2007).

Energy Expenditure of Women: Collection of Fuel and fodder demand great deal of time and energy from women and girls. The 11th Plan document has acknowledged the fact, but in reality nothing significant is done in terms of priority alternative to bio-fuels that causes smoke related illnesses.

Social Security for Women in Informal Sector: The bill on Social Security for women workers, introduced in the parliament has been shelved. In the labour market, bizarre scenario is created where girl children are trafficked for sex trade/ domestic work and slave labour in occupationally hazardous condition, sex exploitation, domestic work/ servitude; young women workers in Special Economic Zone are hired and fired as per the whims of employers and are paid miserable wages. Comprehensive legislation for Protection of Domestic Workers applicable throughout the country is needed urgently. Reasons for non-utilisation of funds under Maternity Benefit Scheme must be examined and concerned offices must be made accountable. In Unorganized *Workers'* Social Security Act, 2008 (Bill No. LXVII of 2008), special problems of women unorganized workers must be included.

Women's Rights Education: No efforts are made by the state or professional bodies for employers' education about basic human rights of women workers. Supreme Court directive on 'prevention of sexual harassment at workplace' is still not implemented by most of the private sector employers and media barons.

Utilisation of Financial Allocation for Pro Women Schemes: Only 3-4 states are taking advantage of financial allocation for Scheme for shelter, clothing and food for women in difficult circumstances, working women's hostel, short stay homes for women in difficult circumstances, UJJAWALA: A Comprehensive Scheme for Prevention of trafficking and Rescue, Rehabilitation and Re-integration of Victims of Trafficking and Commercial Sexual Exploitation. Implementation of crèche scheme is far from satisfactory. Three meals per child per day at the crèches recommended by Eleventh Five Year Plan are rarely provided. Except for Tamil Nadu, Cradle Baby Reception Centres for abandoned babies are non-existent in rest of India. No status report is available on Integrated Child Protection Scheme (ICPS) promised in the Eleventh Five Year Plan.

Fund flow to PRIs has not been streamlined even after separate budgetary allocation for PRIs made in the union budget for past 3 years. How many states have provided women's component in the funds earmarked for the local self-government bodies at village, block and district levels? Is it utilized judiciously for fulfilling practical and strategic needs of women?[1]

Road and Rail Transport for Women: India is undergoing U-shape phenomenon so far as women's work participation is concerned. Most of the working women in urban and rural areas travel in overcrowded buses and trains. In the transport sector top priority needs to be given for women special buses and trains in all cities. For women street vendors, seat-less buses and special luggage compartments in trains need to be provided.

Implementation of Legislations

Promise of the 11th Five Year Plan to allocate funds for Implementation of Pre-Conception and Pre-Natal Diagnostic Test Act (2002) and Domestic Violence Act (2005) has remained unfulfilled in most of the states, and marginally fulfilled in some states such as A.P., Kerala, Karnataka and Tamil Nadu.

No progress is made in providing audit of land and housing rights of women by any ministry-Urban Development, Rural Development, Tribal Development, PRIs and Urban local self Government bodies.

After consistent highlighting of the findings of Rajendrá Sachar Committee Report, 2007 on the deplorable socio-economic status of majority of Muslims in India, special budgetary allocation for socially excluded minority communities is made. In sub-plan for minorities where allocation of Rs. 513 crore[2] is made in Budget Estimates, no specific allocations is made for minority women/ female headed households by Ministry of Minority Affairs.

Inadequate allocation for crucial schemes affecting survival struggles of women such as Rajiv Gandhi National Creche Scheme for Children of Working Mothers (Rs. 56.50 crore), Working Women's Hostel (Rs. 5 crore), Swadhar (Rs. 15 crore), Rescue of victims of trafficking (Rs. 10 crore), Conditional cash transfer for Girl child (for the 1st time introduced and allocation of Rs. 15 crore made) need to be analysed (Nakray, 2009).

Dangerous consequences of tax free clinical trials with stated goal of making India a preferred destination for drug testing to private sector should be taken note of as it will make the poor guinea pigs at the hands of commercial minded techno-docs. Non-utilization and partial utilization of funds allocated for protective, promotive, economic and social welfare programmes for women due to faulty design of the scheme (Maternity Benefits Scheme, non-syncronisation of financial allocation and schemes (funds targeted for adolescent girls' nutrition) and MPLADS (Members of Parliament Area Development scheme) and funds earmarked for grain banks in the tribal areas known for starvation deaths demand urgent attention of politicians, bureaucrats, citizens organizations and women's groups.

Studies need to be commissioned to highlight the gap between plan outlay and outcome, local and global implications of pro-poor and pro-women budgeting, alternative macro scenarios emerging out of alternative budgets and inter-linkages between gender-sensitive budgeting and women's empowerment.

There is an urgent need to sensitise economists about visibility of women in statistics and indicators by holding conceptually and technically sound training workshops by gender economists.

Gender economists have strongly recommended tax reduction for working, self employed and business women. Lowering tax rates for women will put more money in their hands and encourage those not yet in the job market to join the work force. Similarly, property tax rules should be amended further to encourage ownership of assets among women. When women are economically independent and secure, they can exercise choice, enabling them to get out of repressive conditions. Moreover, they would contribute more to our growing economy, making it a win-win situation.

Ministry of Women and Child Development needs more vociferous and visionary leadership, political will and courage of conviction to strive to not only fulfill the promises made by the Eleventh Five Year Plan but also expand the democratic space for women and girls in socio-cultural, economic, educational and political spheres.

Case Study of Union Budget of India, 2010-2011

In the current Union Budget 2010-2011 by the Ministry of Finance of the Government of India, the Women and Child Development Ministry has received an additional allocation of Rs. 2,446 crores over Rs. 7,218 crores in 2009-10. National Mission for Empowerment of Women has been the new initiative this year. The ICDS platform is being expanded for effective implementation of the Rajiv Gandhi Scheme for Adolescent girls. Barring for these encouraging aspects, the current budget has not brought great hopes for women.

The financial allocation for the National Commission for Women that is an apex body for women's empowerment has been reduced from 9.06 to 7.75 crores. The budgetary allocation for working women's hostels is highly inadequate with an increase of only 5 crores at a time when the number of working women is continuously increasing. The Rashtriya Mahila Kosh allocation has come down from 20 to 15 crores that will cast serious blow to livelihoods for women. Leaving this crucial area to financial market will further increase the vulnerability of women's self help groups.

It is shocking to know that the budget provides shamefully low expenditure for relief and rehabilitation for victims of rape. Whereas the allocation was 53.10 crores in the previous budget, the actual expenditure was only 16 lakhs, and the current budgetary outlay has been reduced to 36.2 crores. Yet again, there has been no allocation in the central budget for providing infrastructure, etc, for the Protection of Women from Domestic Violence Act, 2005.

The budget has reduced food subsidy of over 400 crores and the fertilizer subsidy by 3000 crores. The need for a stronger public distribution system to combat widespread hunger and malnutrition which has been the demand of women's organizations has been completely ignored. In fact, the government seems inclined to move towards a dismantling of the existing PDS, to be substituted by food coupons, which can only mean further exclusion of women and the BPL population from food security.

The mid day meal scheme has seen an increase of 16 per cent in the budget, but in the context of a 20 per cent rate of inflation, neither full coverage, nor minimum quality can be ensured. This will further exacerbate the malnutrition status of women and children, particularly those from already marginalized sections like adivasis and Scheduled Castes. The increase for ICDS is 461 crores- which is just about enough to cover existing centres, and cannot provide for the 14 lakh anganwadis to become functional, as per the Supreme Court directive.

While the announcement of the Matritva Sahayog Yojna to assist pregnant and lactating mothers is welcome, the allocations for health and education fall far short of women's groups' demand that each of these ministries should account for 6 per cent of the GDP. There is no mention of the ASHA worker, and no fund allocation to ensure just wages to this woman health activist.

An escalation in prices of essential commodities with the increase in the excise duty on petroleum and petroleum products by Rs. 1.00 per litre will increase the retail prices of petrol and diesel by more than Rs. 2.00 per litre. It will place an additional heavy burden on the shoulders of common women already reeling under an 18% rate of inflation in the last few months.

In its Pre-budget memorandum submitted to the Finance Minister, WomenPowerConnect had stated that in all metropolises-class I, II, III, IV and V cities-safe public transport in terms of buses and trains must be provided to working women. For women vendors and traders, luggage compartments in the trains and buses should be provided. Budget has completely ignored this demand.

In the Budget, 2010-11, the basic threshold limit for income tax exemption will remain at Rs. 1.60 lakh. Under the new proposal, 10 per cent tax will be levied between Rs. 1,60,001 and Rs. 5,00,000, 20 per cent on incomes between Rs. 5,00,001 and Rs. 8,00,000 and 30 per cent above Rs. 8,00,000. For women, the tax exemption will remain at Rs. 1.9 lakh as it was in the previous year's budget.

An analysis of the budgetary allocation by Centre for Budget and Governance Accountability (CBGA) has revealed that child development schemes form 97.2% of the WCD ministry's budget. The lion's share is taken up by the Integrated Child Development Scheme (ICDS) leaving only a measly 2.4% for women-related programmes.

Gender Analysis of State Budgets

The findings of the study of NIPFP were discussed in a workshop held on 3rd - 4th October, 2001 in which representatives from the Finance Ministry, Census, State Governments, UN agencies, gender experts and activists participated (Lahiri et al, 2002). Another Workshop on Gender Analysis of State Budgets was convened on 6th December which was also attended by State Secretaries/Directors of the Department of WCD/ Welfare. The workshop concluded that there is a need to analyse State budgets with a gender perspective since the States/UTs account for bulk of the expenditure in social sector which impinges on the welfare, development and empowerment of women. A network of research institutes and gender experts throughout the country were selected to guide the exercise of analyzing State budgets to track the gender differentiated impact and outcome of budgetary process and policies. The workshop also agreed to a framework for undertaking State level gender budget analysis. It was decided that a quick desk analysis of the State budget documents be made to identify the following categories of schemes and programmes: *Women Specific Schemes* – defined as schemes where 100% of allocation was meant for women; *Pro* Women schemes defined as those, which incorporate at least 30% of allocation for women or significantly benefit women; *Gender-neutral schemes* meant for the community as a whole. These programmes were further classified in four categories on the basis of their potential impact on women's social position: *Protective services,* such as allocations on women's homes and care institutions, rehabilitation schemes for victims of atrocities, pensions for widows and destitute women etc which are aimed at mitigating the consequences of women's social and economic subordination, rather than addressing the root causes of this subordination. *Social services,* such as schemes for education and health of women, support services like crèche and hostels and also water supply sanitation and schemes on fuel and fodder, which contribute significantly to women's empowerment, either directly by building their capacities and ensuring their material well-being, or indirectly through reducing domestic drudgery. *Economic services,* such as schemes for training and skill development, and provision for credit, infrastructure, marketing etc. which are critical to women's economic independence and autonomy. *Regulatory services* which include institutional mechanisms for women's empowerment, such as State Commissions for Women, women's cells in Police Stations, awareness generation programme etc which provide institutional spaces and opportunities for women's empowerment. During the last decade compilations have been made on: Scheme-wise/Sector-wise/Year-wise Budget Estimates/Revised Estimates/ Actual Expenditure in both Plan and Non-Plan Heads; The percentage of Budget Estimates/Revised Estimates/ Actual Expenditure in relation to total budget in both Plan and Non-Plan Heads and also in relation to total social sector budget in both Plan and Non-Plan Head; The percentage of gap between Budget Estimates and Revised Estimates and between Revised Estimates and Actual Expenditure in both Plan and Non-Plan Heads in various identified schemes.

Problem of Utilisation of Funds Allocated for Area Development

In 2006, The Ministry of Women and Child Development was formed. Still for most of the schemes and programmes, there is 66% utilization of financial resources due to faulty designs, antipathy of some state governments and bureaucratic bungling. If the funds remain unutilized, in the subsequent year the allocation is slashed. In several states, funds allocated to women from minority communities whose socio-economic and educational profile is most deplorable, have not been utilised at all! Rs. 2 crores is allocated to each M.P. for the development of the constituency as per Member of Parliament Local Area development Scheme (MPLADS). Utilisation of government funding is the maximum in the North- Eastern states because of strong horizontal and vertical networking. The prosperous states depend more on the private funding to avoid bureaucratic hassles. If poorer areas in the state do not have a highly motivated administration or an NGO network, then too the funding remains unutilised. In the areas dominated by the lower middle class and the poverty groups, there are demands for more schools, libraries, bridges, toilets, drains, tube wells, community centres and crematorium. While in the prosperous areas, the demands are for road repairs and schools. Private sector of the economy demands banks, hospitals and shopping plaza. The (Members of Parliament) M.P. and M.L.A. (Members of Legislative Assembly) have to strike balance by keeping into consideration immediate needs and long-term considerations for the constituency.

To check corruption and bring in transparency in the implementation of rural development projects sponsored by the union government, the Union Rural Development ministry had asked all District Rural Development Agencies (DRDAs) to keep their funds only in the nationalised banks. It has also been made compulsory for the district rural bodies to record complete details of expenditure incurred by them under different heads. People's participation in monitoring the progress of implementation and the mechanism of social audit will also be introduced as part of the new strategy to cleanse the working of the DRDAs (CBGA, 2007). NGOs and Citizens organisations are using Right to Information Act to track proper unitisation of the financial allocation from tax payers' money.

Financial Matters and Local Self Government Bodies (LSGBs)

A recent survey of panchayats working in 19 states, conducted by the National Institute of Rural Development, Hyderabad suggested that LSGBs remain toothless because functional and financial autonomy has not been granted to the PRIs. The study by the Institute of Social Sciences shows that the extent of fiscal decentralisation through the empowerment of PRIs has been very little. The report of the working group on decentralisation appointed by the Karnataka Government has been criticised severely because, "It betrays utter lack of trust in the people which is the keystone of decentralised democracy." (Bandyopadhyay, 2002). Case studies of Panchayat finances in the Gram Sabhas of Midnapur district of West Bengal have corroborated the above-mentioned facts in terms of lack of fiscal autonomy, neglect of girls' education, resource crunch. But it has played substantial role in development of infrastructure, for example rural roads, drinking water, health, education, irrigation and power (Sau, 2002).

Elected representatives, officials at districts and NGOs working in the area should act as facilitators in preparation of the plan for area development and social justice ((Pal, 2002). The UN system has supported allocation of resources for women in PRIs, right from the beginning. "The evidence on gender and decentralisation in India thus suggests that while women have played a positive role in addressing, or attempting to address a range of practical gender needs, their impact on strategic gender needs is not remarkable." (UNDP, 2002). The most challenging task is to enhance capacity of the elected representatives in LSGB to spend funds for community development.

Demands of Women's Groups and Gender Economists

The women's groups are aware that concerns of women cannot be addressed through the Ministry of Women and Child Development alone. It is on the work of women that success of several sectors rest. The changing demographics of agriculture, with more than 75% of all women workers, 85% of rural women workers are in agriculture; women's disproportionately large contribution to the export and services sector, in the unorganised sectors —all these need to be located in the policies. Each of these sectors needs to make concerted efforts to address women's concerns through: recognising women's contributions, addressing their gender specific concerns and organising their voice; investing in skills of women and upgrading their work spaces and providing common work facilities; providing women access to new technologies and credit schemes; paying special attention to caste and minority derived exclusion within gender. Hence, it is important to prioritize universalisation of Gender budgeting (including gender audit) and Gender outcome assessment in all Ministries/Departments at Central and State levels. The Gender Budget Cells located in the different ministries need to be strengthened so that women's concerns can be mainstreamed across different sectors. Further, it needs to be ensured that each of such measures (as listed above) is backed with adequate resource allocation. Calling for implementation of the WCP across all ministries could ensure at least a minimum resource allocation targeted at women. The poor and even receding implementation of WCP as pointed by the Mid Term Appraisal of the Tenth Plan warrants special efforts at correction.

Considering the large numbers of women in unpaid work and women's central role to the care economy; to address women's concerns in these sectors, policies need to focus on social services to support women's care roles (old age, child care). With increasing women's role in the care economy (both paid and unpaid), adequate resource allocations need to be made to support women's care roles. In the absence of sex disaggregated data, evaluation of schemes through a gender lens or any effort at strengthening gender dimensions of existing schemes poses a big question. So, provision of such data should be prioritized. In the light of the present agrarian crisis and the changing face of agriculture being highly gendered, the vulnerability of women farmers in particular needs attention in the larger context of food security.

Considering the huge gender disparities in land ownership patterns, women's access to land needs to be strengthened immediately. This could be done by (a) improving women's claims to family land (by enhancing legal awareness on inheritance laws, provide legal support services, etc.), (b) improving access to public land by ensuring that all land transfers for poverty alleviation, resettlement schemes, etc., recognize women's claims; etc., (c) Improving women's access to land via market through provision of subsidized credit to poor, by encouraging group formation for land purchase or lease by poor women, etc.

Women's rights organizations in India have demanded that the Government should ensure adequate gender budgeting in all ministries and departments, enact a comprehensive Food Security Bill, ensure universal PDS as a core component, allocate 6% of GDP for Health, allocate 6% of GDP for Education, make budgetary allocation to cover special schemes for women workers, increase allocation for women farmers, enhance resource allocation for tribal, dalit, and minority women and increase budgetary support for schemes to assist women-headed households and differently abled women.

The target of 30% gender allocations under all ministries has not yet been achieved. This must be implemented immediately. There is need for gender audit and gender outcome appraisal of all ministries and departments at the central and state levels. Very often, resource allocations made under gender budgeting do not reach in time and they remain unspent. There should be proper monitoring and supervision of the allocated funds with greater transparency and accountability at all levels.

Conclusion

Budget audit from the perspective of poor, women, minorities, people with disability, children, geriatric groups and other vulnerable sections is now practised by many countries with an objective to support government and civil society in examining national, regional and local budgets from a sectional perspective and applying the study results for the formulation of responsive budgets. There is no single approach or model of a sensitive budget exercise. In some countries, for example, these exercises are implemented by the government while in other countries individuals and groups outside government undertake the budgetary analysis.

Budgets garner resources through the taxation policies and allocate resources to different sections of the economy. There is a need to highlight participatory approaches to pro-poor budgeting, bottom up budget, child budget, SC budget, ST budget, green budgeting, local and global implications of pro-poor and pro-women budgeting, alternative macro scenarios emerging out of alternative budgets and inter-linkages between gender-sensitive budgeting and women's empowerment (Bhat et al, 2004). Bottom up budgets have emerged as an important and widespread strategy for scrutinizing government budgets for their contribution to marginalised sections of economy. They have utilized a variety of tools and processes to assess the impact of government expenditures and revenues on the social and economic position of men, women, boys and girls. Serious examination of budgets calls for greater transparency at the level of international economics to local processes of empowerment. There is a need to provide training and capacity building workshops for decision-makers in the government structures, gram sabhas, parliamentarians and audio-visual media (Patel, 2004).

Budget analysis from gender perspective should be introduced and promoted in all women's groups, educational and research institutions. Public debate on gender sensitive budget will help the country to tilt the balance in favour of area development and peaceful use of resources in the present atmosphere of jingoism. Gender commitments must be translated into budgetary commitment. By using the Right to Information (2005), transparency /accountability for revenue generation and public expenditure can be ensured. For Reprioritisation in public spending we must prepare 'bottom up budgets' and lobby for its realisation in collaboration with the elected representatives. Gender economists must lift the veil of statistical invisibility of the unpaid 'care economy' managed by poor women and highlight equality & efficiency dimension and transform macro-policies so that they become women friendly.

The gender budget initiative has opened new vistas of research and analysis of public expenditure in the country and opened serious methodological debates for carrying out such analysis. This has also highlighted the urgency of sharpening the methodological tools for monitoring the progress of Women's Component Plan introduced in the Ninth Five Year Plan. Efforts at ensuring gender-just and gender-sensitive budget demands continuous process of dissecting the government budget to establish its gender-differential impact and translation of gender commitment to budgetary commitments- Outlay of Rs. 13,780 crores and Women Component Plan and Gender Budget to play complimentary role for effective convergence, proper utilisation and monitoring of fund from various developmental sectors.

Notes

1. Strategic Gender Needs are different in different economic contexts and are determined by statutory provisions, affirmative

action by the state, pro-active role of the employers to enhance women's position in the economy and social movements. Practical Gender Needs are identified keeping in consideration, gender based division of labour or women's subordinate position in the economy. They are a response to immediate perceived necessity, identified within a specific context. They are practical in nature and often are concerned with inadequacies in living conditions such as provision of fuel, water, healthcare and employment.

2. 1 crore = 10 million.

References

Bandopadhyaya, D. 2002, "Panchayats in Karnataka", *Economic and political Weekly*, 37:35, August 31- September 6, pp. 3572-3573.

Banerjee, N. 2002, "What is Gender Budgeting?" Public Policies from Women's Perspective in the Indian Context, UNIFEM- United Nations Development Fund for Women, Delhi. Website- http://www.unifem.org.in

Banerjee, N. and Roy, P. 2004, "What Does the State Do for Indian Women?" *Economic and Political Weekly*, Review of Women Studies, 39:44, October 30-November 5, pp. 4831-4837.

Bhat, A., Kolhar, S., Chellappa, A. and H. Anand 2004, "Building Budgets from Below", *Economic and Political Weekly*, Review of Women Studies, 39:44 October 30-November 5, pp. 4803-4810.

CBGA (2007), Budget 2007-08: Dream or Despair? Response to the Union Budget 2007-08, Centre for Budget and Governance Accountability (CBGA), Delhi.

Lahiri, A., Chakraboorty, L. and Bhattacharya, P.N. 2002, "Gender Budgeting in India", The National Institute of Public Finance ad Policy, New Delhi.

Nakray, K. 2009, "Gender Budgeting: Does it Really Work? Some Experiences from India", U.K. : *Policy and Politics*, Vol. 37, No. 2, pp. 307-10.

Patel, V. 2002, *Women's Challenges of the New Millennium*, Gyan Publishing House, Delhi.

Patel, V. 2009, http://www.gender-budgets.org/content/view/292/156/ United Nations Development Fund for Women (UNIFEM) and The Commonwealth Secretariat.

Rajaram, I. 2007, "Women in the Eleventh Plan", National Institute of Public Finance and Policy, Delhi.

Sau, S. 2002, "Decentralised Financial and Physical Planning: A Study across Gram Panchayats and Blocks in Midnapore District of West Bengal", Department of Economics with Rural Development, Vidyasagar University, Midnapur, West Bengal.

UNDP 2001, *Decentralisation in India- Challenges and Opportunities*, United Nations development programme, New Delhi.

4

From Krupabai Satthianadhan to Shashi Deshpande: Mapping the Journey of the Feminist Novel in India

Sumita Parmar

"For a woman, intelligence is always a burden, Indu. We like our women not to think."

Roots and Shadows (33)

This chapter looks at the journey of the novel written in English by Indian women. Providing a brief social and historical context, it examines how from the first publication in 1894 of Krupabai Satthianadhan's novel, it evolved responding to and reflecting the profound changes taking place in the country. Surveying the growth of the novel in the post-Independence period, the chapter moves to contemporary times. It focuses on well-known and respected writer Shashi Deshpande's novel *Roots and Shadows* demonstrating how it is a significant feminist novel.

From the year 1894, when the first novel in English written by an Indian woman was published, to contemporary times, the novel has traversed a long and eventful distance. This chapter investigates the journey in India that such a novel has made and examines its changing avatars during this 116 years old journey. More than any other literary form, the novel mirrors the events that happen in society. It imbibes the changes that are affected, reflects how they transform social structures, shows how mindsets evolve and transform, how history impacts people and in a dynamic process how the novel is itself created and transformed by the very processes it reflects. It has been frequently said about great novels that they are more accurate in their depiction and rendering of the social realities of their times than historical or economic and even sociological and anthropological books. Thus novels are and become socio –cultural 'documents' fulfilling more roles than just literary.

Since education is fundamentally connected to the writing and creation of literature, a very brief look at how formal education for women was introduced in India and how it took roots in the country will not only give a sense of perspective, but will also provide a true measure of the kind of progress women have made in the last century.

It is important to bear in mind that till the eighteenth century women were not educated, except in the affairs of the house in order to become good wives and mothers. Even by the nineteenth century, hardly any progress had been made and women were generally illiterate and subjugated by all manner of social constraints. When the Britishers came, initially they were reluctant to interfere with the established cultural and religious codes and existing social structures. They wanted to be perceived as people who were primarily interested in trade and not as arrogant outsiders who presumed to improve existing and age old traditions. Of all the castes, the Brahmins were the most hostile to the English since they perceived them as a threat to their hegemony. As caste categorizations were made and recorded, various groups had made continuous efforts at upward mobility and the Brahmins had thwarted these with matching resistance. However, the inputs that the British got from various sources including their officials gave them the impression that, "the situation in India was so appalling that it called for an intervention by an ethical and rational power. The British quickly persuaded themselves that India was the white man's burden and their government essential to their salvation" (Tharu & Lalitha, 1991:9). Consequently, as the nature of the British presence in the country began to change, so did the power alignments and social configurations. In this whole process, gender became a crucial component in the stakes and claims made by the various castes. The stricter the gender codes were in a caste, the higher their claims to superiority were. In other words, the prestige of the caste /community was put on the shoulders of the women. Thus the Brahmins, who claimed the highest / purest status, had the most stringent gender codes for their women and the customs for the enforced widowhood were also the strictest in their case. Cutting across caste/community lines, all attempts at educating girls and women were viewed with hostility and opposition:

> The central concern with protection of female sexuality and the attendant notions of female purity/impurity and its links to caste status and the honour of the agnatic kingroup and familial considerations put severe constraints on the education of girls and women (Rege, 2003:288).

Bu; the importance of education for women in attaining a better status and leading better lives could not be overstated. The social reformers of the early nineteenth century laid down the foundations of the reform movements upon which those following them could build. They showed great courage and persistence in their efforts and often had to face excommunication from their castes and communities. In such a context, whatever progress was made in promoting the education and emancipation of women was very significant and achieved at great cost. In fact, in Bengal there was so much hostility to the idea of women's education when it was first introduced that rumours were started claiming women became masculine if they were educated! (Saxena, 2007:21-31). Maharashtra, Bengal and Kerala were in the vanguard of the movement to emancipate women and the developments in these regions generally found their way to the other parts of the country.

It is interesting to note the complicity of the women in their own subordination. The cultural conditioning was so deep that the women became the agents of their own and the disempowerment of other women. For example, it was Gopal Hari Deshmukh's daughter's mother-in-law who threatened to dissolve the marriage of her son if he went ahead with the remarriage of a widow (Chakravarti, 1998:93). This sense of sublimation in their personal disempowerment lingers on as a mindset in many women even in our times.

Given this fact, that women could access proper education only from the nineteenth century, their contribution to literature remains comparatively small. However, remarkable strides have been taken in the passing years and the volume and variety of writings by women novelists has increased manifold.

(I)

The credit for being the first Indian woman to have written a novel in English goes to Krupabai Sattianadhan who was born in a Maharashtrian family in 1862. She was an outstanding woman who dedicated her short life to educating girls. The novel was called *Saguna-A Story of a Native Christian Life* (1894). Her second novel was entitled *Kamala-A Study of H ndu Life*.(1895) During the same period Rajalakshmi Devi wrote *The Hindu Wife* (1876) which was followed by Toru Dutt's *Bianca* (1878.) Although these novels were critical of society, especially those aspects which concerned women, their tones were mild and gently chastising. In the early part of the twentieth century, Begum Rokeya Sakhawat Hussain (1880-1932) published *Sultana's Dream* (1905). Like Krupabai, she, too, was actively involved in the education of women and her novel is clearly feminist in attitude and content. She refuted the widespread assumption that women were held in high honour in traditional Hindu and Muslim society. In 1901, Cornelia Sorabji wrote *Love and Life Behind the Purdah,* also called *Purdanasheen,* which gave a description of life behind purdah.

As the fight for Independence gained momentum, a nationalist discourse evolved which privileged the achievement of Independence over all other issues including those regarding women. However, after Independence was won, several women writers emerged who articulated the fundamental concerns regarding the position of women in the newly formed nation. Prominent among them were Kamala Markandaya (*Nectar in a Sieve*,1954, *Some Inner Fury*,1957, *Silence of Desire,* 1961, *Possession,* 1963, *A Handful of Rice*,1966, *The Coffer Dams,*1969), Ruth Prawer Jhabvala (*To Whom She Will,*1955,*The Nature of Passion,*1956, *Esmond in India,* 1958, *The House Holder* 1960, *Get Ready for Battle,*1962, *A Backward Place,1965*), Anita Desai (*Cry the Peacock*, 1963,*Voices in the City*, 1965, *Bye-Bye Blackbird*, 1971, *Fasting and Feasting*) and Nayantara Sahgal (*A Time to be Happy,*1957 and *This Time of Morning,* 1965). Each of these novelists, with a substantial volume of work had distinct approaches and choice of themes. While economic, political and spiritual frameworks housed Markandya's plots, Jhabvala focused on relationships, and the interaction between people belonging to different cultural backgrounds against the backdrop of Partition and political upheavals. Desai's was and remains an interior canvas and she concentrates on analysis and the sensibilities of the characters. Sahgal, too, writes within the framework of politics and the newly acquired political freedom. There were others as well such as Santha Rama Rau (*Remember The House*, 1956), Shakuntala Sriganesh (*The Little Black Box,* 1955), Attia Hosain (*Sunlight on a Broken Column*, 1961), but each of them wrote only a single novel.

The Women's Movement of the 1960s in the West saw the publication of a number of books which are considered seminal texts for feminists. Simone de Beauvior's *The Second Sex,*(1950), Kate Millet's *Sexual Politics,* Betty Friedan's *The Feminine Mystique* and Germaine Greer's *The Female Eunuch* were all written in the 1960s and deeply influenced the perceptions of women all over the world. India was no exception and there was a marked upsurge in the novels written by women accompanied by a distinct change in the treatment of women's issues and the kind of themes that began to be written about. Topics which were taboo earlier like the acknowledgement of women's sexuality and her sexual needs, questions of autonomy and the need for assertion, a desire for selfhood and the will to concretize that desire, the discontent in marriage, unreasonable social expectations, all these began to be articulated in the fiction being written by the post 1960s writers. Novelists like Shobha De and Namita Gokhale wrote with a frankness about female sexuality, a frankness which some found disconcerting. Others like Githa Hariharan, a feminist contemporary novelist, wrote with sensitivity regarding the relationships of men and women and the politics of power which colour them. In *A Thousand Faces of Night,* which won the Commonwealth Writers Prize for the Best First Novel in 1992, Hariharan portrays three generations of women—a daughter, a mother and their maid. The novel describes the subtle and not so subtle ways in which women face erasure.

The revisiting of ancient texts and new ways of interpreting them form an important part of the writing of many of the women novelists of today. Myths are given new faces, old tales shrouded in tradition are re-examined, questioned, sometimes exposed in their subterfuge and the hidden agendas they promote and reinforce. The more assertive versions of the story of Sita find their way into contemporary writings and are rendered in newer forms. Gail Omvedt states in Dalit Visions:

> ...beyond the Valmiki Ramayana, and its even more patriarchal successors (such as the Tulsidas Ramayana, which brought in the theme of the *lakshman rekha*) we find in Sita, inclinations to rebel. Some traditions depict her love for Ravana (indicating perhaps that this may be a subterranean theme of even the orthodox version in which she is only suspected). There is strong peasant-based tradition of Sita that emphasizes her rejection of Rama after she has been sent away, her anger at the injustices done to her. In a folk poem of Uttar Pradesh, for instance, Sita refuses to go back even when Lakshman has been sent to bring her, and instead raises her sons on her own and gives them her father's name, in a half-way return to matriliny. The Thai version of the Ramayana, similarly, ends with Sita refusing to go back until the gods themselves intervene to restore family propriety (Omvedt, 1995: 99).

(II)

Of the numerous writers on the Indian scene, Shashi Deshpande is one whose oeuvre addresses the most fundamental issues regarding women vis-à-vis themselves and women vis-à-vis society. A highly esteemed writer, Deshpande's first novel, *The Dark Holds No Terrors* was published in 1980. Since then she has written steadily, her work covering short stories and essays too. Her latest novel *Country of Deceit* came out in 2008, bringing the total number of her novels to nine. She won the prestigious Sahitya Akademi Award in 1990 for her novel *That Long Silence* and was awarded the Padma Shri Award in 2009. Deshpande writes with a deep empathy and perception about women focusing especially on the life of the urban educated, middle-class woman. The challenge of balancing tradition and modernity, home and profession and at the same time finding the self and 'of becoming'— as it is referred to these days—these are what constitute her themes. She has stated her feelings regarding several issues related to women, society, traditions, religion both in her essays and in the interviews she has given. These help enhance the understanding of her works and underline the issues close to her heart.

Jasbir Jain, well-known critic writes, "The woman writer has to decide for herself how far she wants to deromanticise the image created by men and also how to use her anger and resentment towards positive ends. Part of the struggle lies also in the need to outgrow the socially propagated and individually internalised patriarchal values. She has addressed these problems in various ways and through different situations just as she has grown into new awareness" (Jain, 2003: 14). In her book entitled *Writings from the Margin and other essays* she is emphatic about the debt that she and all women owe to the feminists. She states, 'I have no doubt at all that it is the women's movement which has made it possible for an increasing number of women to have more space to breathe. I know that as a writer I am privileged to be living at a time when the women's movement has made it possible for my voice to be heard, for the things I write about to be taken seriously, looked upon as issues that concern all of society, and not just dismissed as 'women's stuff" ...(Deshpande, 2003: 83).

Deshpande's work reverberates with the issues that are of central concern to not only avowed feminist activists, but to anyone who is concerned about the well-being of society and all its members. Firmly rooted in home and family it nevertheless spans issues which involve the larger world. Thus the microcosm that is the family is a reflection of the macrocosm that is the world outside it. Addressing the perennial questions of selfhood, compatibility, loyalty, love, hate and jealousy, power relations, what drives people to attain power, what it does to them, the importance of money and its impact on the lives of those who have it as well as those who do not, her work locates and contextualizes these universals within the protean framework of the family which could be large joint family or a small nuclear one.

It seems to have become almost fashionable these days for women to say that they are not feminists, but Deshpande makes her statement in ringing tones. Without being strident, her statement about why she is a feminist makes a case for the kind of feminism that is positive and constructive rather than one that is divisive and destructive. Says she:

> It took me years to say even to myself. 'I am a feminist.' It was the culmination of a voyage that began within myself and went on to the ocean of women's place in the world. Today, when I call myself a feminist, I believe that the female of the species has the same right to be born and survive, to fulfill herself and shape

> her life according to her needs and the potential that lies within her, as the male has. I believe that women are neither inferior nor subordinate human beings, but one half of the human race. I believe that women (and men as well) should not be straitjacketed into roles that warp their personalities, but should have options available to them. I believe that Nature, when conferring its gifts on humans, did not differentiate between males and females, except for the single purpose of procreation. I believe that motherhood does not bar everything else, but is a bonus, an extra that women are privileged to have. Would the anti-feminists deny all this? (Ibid: 83).

The questions that Deshpande raises in her novels are germane to women everywhere but in the Indian sub-continent, bound as it is by a similarity of cultures and values, they become specially meaningful and easy for women to identify with.

Marriage, power relations within the larger family— the politics that thrives and is practiced within its confines, the women who are sometimes adroit and astute manipulators of others and sometimes victims, sometimes astute judges of characters, perceptive and ruthless, and sometimes perpetrators of their own subjugation, the men, sometimes frustrated and helplessly caught in the system, and sometimes indifferent, selfish and arrogant—all the drama that is played out at a national level is repeated and reflected on a smaller scale in the family and Deshpande is, with her keen observations and neutral voice, an impressive narrator of these tales.

In novel after novel, in recurring frameworks of joint families, her protagonists are confronted with situations where they are compelled to address issues which demand that they step out of their comfort zones and make decisions for which they are accountable. The basic fact that they are forced to come to terms with is, that in the final count, they are accountable to themselves and however much they might be tempted to blame others, in spite of all the constraints, a certain degree of accountability cannot be wished away. Shashi Deshpande's radicalism is quiet in nature, located within the traditional and conventional framework of the family and domesticity. Her heroines do not divorce or runaway from the situations they find themselves in but make radical decisions, which may or may not be discernible outside, but which nevertheless transform and work from within helping the protagonists evolve and move towards selfhood.

(III)

Although *That Long Silence* is one of her most acclaimed novels and the *Country of Deceit* her latest, it is *Roots and Shadows*, one of her earliest novels, published in 1983 that is the most radical and subversive both in its content and treatment of the theme of family and power. In this work, Deshpande turns established traditional systems on their heads. The contested sites in the majority of her novels are the family, marriage and the self. The dramas and action which the characters participate in and the uncertainties, frustrations and doubts they have to negotiate occur in them. *Roots and Shadows* is no exception and family, marriage and selfhood constitute the fundamental components of the story. In it the novelist explores many of the themes that are integral to her concerns and which she has voiced often. The tone of the novel is set in the opening chapter when Indu tells Mini, who is to get married, that she should 'forget the rules for a change.'

The story is about a traditional Brahmin joint family living in a sprawling house which has seen better days. One of the senior-most members of the family, a rich grand–aunt, Akka, is dying and decides to give away her money to a grand-niece, Indu who is the protagonist of the novel. Indu is a writer who had left several years ago, married a man of her own choice and thus earned the disapproval of the family. She is summoned by Akka and on arrival, to her utter surprise and dismay she learns of her grand-aunt's decision. The plot is essentially about the consequences of this unexpected move. Encased within this story are other stories in multiple time frames.

With an open mind and an ability to question old traditions, Indu is one of the strongest characters that Deshpande has created. She thinks out of the box, has the confidence to go against her relatives, many of who are senior and higher than her in the domestic hierarchy, handles money with wisdom and without greed, and has sex outside marriage without feeling overtly guilty about it. Indeed, Indu manifests all the qualities of not only a liberated woman but of a sound and liberated human being.

In a rigidly patriarchal system Akka leaves her wealth to a young woman, her grand-niece. By handing over her money to Indu rather than to the many senior and older male members of the family, Akka gives her the power to decide the fate of many members of the family. Interestingly, the family members come to terms with this unusual situation rather quickly. Perhaps, it is because of fact that Indu has been away from the family for many years that Akka thinks the distance will help her handle the family responsibility better than the man who are around who, Akka is not confident, will not be swayed by their personal biases. As she grapples with the decisions that she has to make regarding the way the money is going to be spent, and whether the old house has to be sold or not, Indu finds herself asking the question, 'what would Akka have done?' The thought of the old woman and her ability to make decisions without being influenced by others and keeping the benefits of the larger family in mind, helps Indu to make some tough decisions herself.

Marriage

The subject of marriage resonates in the work of Shashi Deshpande and constitutes a central theme in her novels. She critiques the institution of marriage as it existed in the past and even as it does today. She is scathing in her portraiture and depicts what this great patriarchal institution requires of women. She narrates the extent to which women have to confine, restrict, remodel and reinvent themselves in order to make their marriages successful.

Thus we have Jaya in *The Long Silence* who thinks of marriage as two animals bound together. In *A Matter of Time,* Gopal simply walks away from his marriage in order to 'find' himself. Why he got married in the first place, remains a mystery. In *The Dark Holds no Terror,* the subject of marital rape is addressed. However, Deshpande does not portray the women in the contemporary marriages, she writes about as victims and places part of the success or failure of the relationship at their door. Thus at the conclusion of *A Long Silence*, Jaya resolves to be more interactive with her husband instead of bottling up her, resentments over the years and letting them embitter, her relationship with him.

Roots and Shadows contains a wide spectrum of marriages— love marriages, arranged ones and marriages of convenience. From the disastrous one of Akka's to the typical one of kaka, the only common ground is the concern of family and children. The novelist strips the institution of all romanticism and lays it bare. Indu, reflecting on the marriage of her cousin Mini thinks:

> Behind the facade of romanticism, sentiment and tradition, what was marriage after all but two people brought together after cold-blooded bargaining to meet, mate and reproduce so that the generations might continue?(3)[1]

A similar sentiment is expressed by Hemant, another cousin married, with two children:

> It's a trap ...that's what marriage is. A trap? Or a cage? Maybe the comic strip version of marriage... a cage with two trapped animals glaring hatred at each other...isn't so wrong after all. And it's not a joke, but a tragedy. But what animal would cage itself ? (60-61)

But to Mini marriage is something quite different. In *That Long Silence,* marriage has been described as a 'sheltering tree' for women and that's what Mini expects it to be for her. It's an escape and a refuge both. It's a fulfillment of her destiny and an entry into a domain of security. 'To her it was marriage that mattered, not the man'(4). Mini represents the woman whose life is circumscribed by rigid expectations and inflexible codes of conduct, the flouting of which results in severe consequence. She has watched helplessly the humiliation that her parents have undergone as they have welcomed what has seemed to be an endless line of prospective bridegrooms and their parents, only to be rejected for some reason or the other. She has been pushed to a point where she will do anything to stop the humiliation—more of her parent's than her own—even if it means marrying an uncultured man with coarse features. She shares her feelings with Indu:

> You don't know what it has been like. Watching Kaka and Hemant and even Madhav-kaka running around after eligible men. And then, sending the horoscope and having it come back with the message, "It doesn't match". And if the horoscopes matched, there was the meeting to be arranged. And mother and Atya slogging in the kitchen the whole day. And all those people coming...and staring and asking all kinds of questions. And if we heard that they were old fashioned people, I would dress up in an old fashioned manner and they would say, "She's not modern enough." And if I dressed up well because someone said that the boy wanted a smart wife, they would say, "She's too fashionable for us". Or too short. Or too tall. Or too dark. Or something. And Kaka trying to laugh and talk to those people while his eyes looked so...anxious. And I, feeling as if I had committed a great crime by being born a girl...And finally if everything was fine, there was the dowry (126).

But if Deshpande is scathing in the portrayal of the traditional marriage, there are happy marriages as well and one of them is that of Indu's parents. 'Ever since I had known it, there had been to me something sacred in the love between my father and mother, who had overcome the then almost unsurmountable barriers of caste and lived a tragically short but intensely happy life together' (75). Even Old Uncle, whose wife Saroja had died fifty years ago, can still recall the happy memories of his marriage. He confides in Indu:

> She was only thirteen, and an ignorant village girl when I married her. And I, a bookish solemn young man, thinking it my duty to educate her. She taught me so much more herself. She knew how to reach across to any person, so easily getting across the barriers of age, class, caste or sex. Mothers-in-law, you know what they are supposed to be. But I think my mother would have attacked me if had said a harsh word to my wife(180).

However, happy marriages are uncommon in Deshpande's novels. Even the protagonist Indu, who has married Jayant, a man of her choice, is dissatisfied with her relationship with her husband since it is unable to give her all that she expects. The impact of Jayant on her is something that she almost reluctantly acknowledges:

> When I look in the mirror, I think of Jayant. When I dress, I think of Jayant. When I undress, I think of him. Always what he wants. What he would like. What would please him. And I can't blame him. It's not he who has pressurized me

> into this. It's the way I want to be. And one day I thought ...isn't there anything I want at all? Have I become fluid, with no shape, no form of my own? ....And a still more frightful, a comically frightful thought had occurred. Am I on my way to becoming an ideal woman? A woman who sheds her 'I', who loses her identity in her husband's? (49).

Analyzing her relationship with her husband, she explains to herself that because she loves him so deeply, indeed, as she ruefully admits to herself, perhaps loves him too much she will only be happy if she scales down her expectations. She ought to expect from Jayant only what he was capable of giving, "deep affection, yes: total absolute commitment, no..." (56).

An objective look at her marriage makes her realize certain facts. "... one day I had realized that what we were saying was... 'Don't judge me. Don't criticize me. Just appreciate me. Only my virtues, not my vices. My strengths, not my weaknesses' This is what we want. And we call it perfect understanding (115)". She also discovers aspects of her self which she did not know existed, aspects that her marriage brings out. One is them being her capacity for deception.

> I had found in myself an immense capacity for deception. I had learnt to reveal to Jayant nothing but what he wanted to see, to say to him nothing but what he wanted to hear. I hid my responses and emotions as if they were bits of garbage (38).

But more than any other, the most traumatic marriage is Akka's and the story is first narrated to Indu by Atya:

She was just twelve when she got married. And he was well past thirty...He was a tall bulky man with large coarse features. And she... she was small and dainty, really pretty, with her round face, fair skin, straight nose and curly hair...What she had to endure there, no one knows. She never told anyone... But twice she tried to run away... a girl of thirteen. Her mother-in-law whipped her for that and locked her up for three days. Starved her as well. And then, sent her back to her husband's room. The child, they said, cried and clung to her mother-in-law saying, "Lock me up again, lock me up."

Her husband had a weakness for women. How could a frightened child satisfy him? He always had mistresses. And Akka could never give birth to a living child. Not surprising, considering the kind of life she lead. But every time she had a miscarriage, her mother-in-law blamed her for it and made life hell for her (70).

The story turns around when the husband suffers a stroke. Atya continues the horrible narrative and recounts how after the terrible stroke when Akka's husband 'couldn't even wiggle a toe' she looked after him and kept him spotless. But she had her revenge for even though he begged in the only way he could through the horrible guttural sounds he could make that he wanted to see his mistress, Akka informed him that the woman had been trying to meet him, that she had come twice to the house and that Akka had ordered that she should be sent away and that now he could never as long as he was alive ever see her and how upon hearing this the man had actually started to cry- "tears poured down his face. He cried like a child. He couldn't even wipe his tears...But Akka, she just looked at him...Calm and cool she said, "Listen to me. It's my turn now. I've listened to you long enough. She came here. Twice. She wanted to see you. She cried and begged to be allowed to see you just for a short while. I threw her out. You'll never see her again" (71). This is the sad and tragic story of the transformation of an innocent and young girl into a cynical, autocratic and ruthless woman who appears to have a heart of stone. It's a horrifying portrait of the kind of marriages that often took place during those times. After her husband's death, Akka becomes a rich woman, comes to live with her brother Anant (Kaka) and wields total authority over the entire family till her death. The story of Akka comes full circle when as an old woman on her deathbed she summons Indu and in the face of the expectations of her male relatives makes her the heiress, the person who would get all the money and therefore, who would be obliged to make decisions normally made by the head of the family. This story within the main story casts a shadow on the entire novel and Akka has a tangible presence even after her death. In a twist of irony, the woman who was so completely sans power at one point in her life, exercises so much of it in the latter part of her life and passes it on in the form of money to another woman. In fact, it is only after she has heard about Akka's history that Indu's respect for her grows, and she realizes how the old woman has subverted the system which made her suffer so much for so long.

Family

In Deshpande's work, the family is a world unto itself, distinct and unique. In its power play and politics it reflects the larger external world. It means diverse things to different people. Thus to some it translates into refuge, security, and identity, while to others it is something which restricts, confines and is to be abandoned. To Indu it means both. As a young infant whose mother died shortly after giving birth to her, she was brought to her father's family where she grew up. "I think of my own childhood, and of how I got affection from Kaka, understanding from Old Uncle. And loving care from Atya; and I know why there is faint tinge of pity in me for the small families of today. Father, Mother, and child...(13). She has memories of contentment and happiness related to the large family of her childhood:

> The enchantment of waking up in the morning to various sounds that somehow formed a harmonious whole. Birds chirping in the windows. A child crying...The Primus hissing. The tinkle of cups and saucers. Akka singing. And then, the magic of the evening hours, when the first lamp was lit for the gods. The lights gently twinkling in all the rooms. Women sitting at ease for the first time in the day, stretching out their aching legs in front of them. Story-telling time... children lying with heads pillowed on warm laps, listening with a drowsy intentness, when the whole didn't matter, but each word was significant and meaningful. Men returning home, shedding their slippers, washing their feet and settling down with large contented sighs. The feeling of ease, contentment and indolence embracing the whole house. And the huge front door, which no child could ever push the whole way, standing wide open the whole day, so that people just walked in and became part of the family. An aura of warmth that didn't have to be

> said in words, smiles, dinner and drinks. This was home. Where one lived. Not stayed (97).

Yet, even as a child Indu had seen the bitterness among family members, "the intrigues, the groups, the schisms in a family. The jealousies, the rivalries, the barbed tongues and malicious words." She can see it even more clearly now that she is grown up and has been away from it all for so many years. She comprehends why she had left in the first place:

> It's this kind of living, I thought. Living too close, too entangled with one another. So that if you move, you are bound to hurt someone else. And if they move they hurt you. So many diverse pulls, so many conflicting feelings. And yet, surprisingly, it was still a family (131).

She sees that "if the family was united at all it was in this... a readiness to revile the others, tours misunderstand, to see the worst" (60) and that there was "envy and bitterness. Greed and anger...a slow smoldering anger. And malice and meaness"(59).

But where she can be critical of the family, Deshpande also draws this tender and charming portrait of what the family can be in its better avatars. The perspective is again Indu's:

> The men and children sitting down to lunch. Rows of plates made of dried leaves woven together, laid from end to end in the large hall, interspersed with supporting pillars of wood....The children, their faces decorously subdued were eagerly waiting to be served. The men were, most of them, without their shirts, as

> was the custom at meals. The sacred thread seemed like a marker between the generations. None of the younger men had it. A commonplace picture: but I felt as if I was looking at something that did not exist, something that was on the brink of dissolution. And it became a thing of beauty, like anything ephemeral. And yet, since coming for the wedding, I had seen the concept of the family taking shape, living, in front of my eyes (59).

Sustained by the myriad invisible sacrifices that the women in it make, the family as an entity makes unending demands on the women in it. Deshpande comments on this institutionalization of the martyred woman, 'If you serve milk and rice to everyone and content yourself with plain rice alone, we shall be able to say that you are the proper daughter of a wise father.' I read these words of a Bengali folksong and wondered—when and where along the way did she become a goddess of self-denial? 'Anything will do for me.' 'I'm not really hungry.' 'If you all are satisfied, I am too. I don't need to eat' (Deshpande, 2003: 141). Service, obedience, loyalty—these are the qualities that women are expected to have in the twin institutions of marriage and family. Not questioning minds or a desire to learn. As Old Uncle tells Indu, "For a woman, intelligence is always a burden, Indu. We like our women not to think" (33). Indu, as other Deshpande protagonists, develops the ability to see the family holistically. It is this ability which enables them to benefit from it. For in the words of Old Uncle, "the family ...it's all right to sneer at it. But tell me what have you got to put in its place? What will you have in its stead? It gives us a background, an anchor, something to hold on to..." (104).

Selfhood and Autonomy

The question of selfhood, when the woman is thinking about herself what she wants to do, or be, or would like, in other words, when she can have an autonomous composite self, is a crucial issue in Deshpande's work. The persona that the married woman, equipped with a brand new name, has to don, the roles that a woman is expected to play, are all so overwhelming that she tends to lose herself, forget what she intrinsically is. The question of retrieving this lost self and countering erasure is what constitutes autonomy and selfhood in this writer's novels.

Indu wonders about the women who are a part of her family, some of whom she loves and who have brought her up. She cannot comprehend them. Bewildered she thinks:

> Kaku ...what was her real name? Perhaps, she had no name at all. These women...they are called kaku and kaki, atya and Vahini, Ajji and Mami. As if they have to be recognized by a relationship, because they have no independent identity of their own at all. And, in the process, their own names are forgotten. How does it feel not even to have a name of your own? There are women who are proud of having their names changed by their husbands during their wedding ceremonies. To surrender your name so lightly....But what's in a name?...after a while the name becomes meaningless, like any other word after constant repetition. As meaningless as Kaku (117).

However, Kaki's surprising outburst while discussing Mini's marriage is indicative of some of the resentments that brew within the women. "Who knows anything about me, child? Has anyone ever asked me what I want? That's why I'm telling you...ask Mini what she wants. It's not good enough, your saying, or her father's saying...let her marry Naren. Ask *her* what *she* wants" (121). Indu thinks of the kind of inner strength the women are required to have to survive and endure:

> A woman's life, they had told me, contained no choices. And all my life, especially in this house, I had seen the truth of this. The women had no choice but to submit, to accept. And I had often wondered...have they been born without will, or have their wills atrophied through a life time of disuse? And yet Mini, who had no choice either, had accepted the reality, the finality, with a grace and composure that spoke eloquently of that inner strength (6).

But for her, being a woman is synonymous with living within constraints, "Yes it was true. I felt hedged in, limited by my sex. I resented my womanhood because it closed so many doors to me" (79). In the confines of the family, being a girl meant only a few limited things, all essentially connected with marriage and procreation. Thus when Indu is told about the physical aspects of what being female meant, her reaction is not surprising. "My womanhood...I had never thought of it until the knowledge had been thrust brutally, gracelessly on me the day I had grown up. 'You're a woman now,' kaki had told me, 'You can have babies yourself'. And then she had gone on to tell me, badly, crudely, how I could have a baby. And I, who had had all the child's unselfconsciousness about my own body, had, for the first time, felt an immense hatred for it" (79).

When Indu leaves her home it is to distance herself from these confinements and attitudes. The measure of her maturity can be assessed by her response to her sexual encounter with Naren. Tucked away innocuously in the story, towards the end of the novel is the episode about Indu and Naren sleeping together. Naren, who is Old Uncle's grandson, is a rebel of sorts, perceptive and unconventional in his attitudes. He and Indu share a bond with each other and use each other as sounding boards. The incident, when it happens, is satisfying and natural to both:

> There was a joyous sense of release, of passion I could experience and show and participate in. I clung to him convulsively, marveling that I did not have to hold myself back. And when it was over, we lay back, both of us, exhausted and shuddering. I said, 'Thank you, Naren' (152).

Later, Indu says to herself, "I don't have to erase anything I have done." However, a lifetime of conditioning cannot be dismissed so easily and inevitably, she confronts the act in her mind:

> And now, I thought, the enormity of what I have done will come home to me. Adultery...what nuances of wrongdoing...no, it needs the other, stronger word...what nuances of sin the word carries. I will now brood on my sin, be crushed under a weight of guilt and misery. But, instead, perversely, my mind began, coldly, analytically, to think of what I had done. I thought of all this with a kind of remorseless logic, a detached objectivity, as if I was thinking of some other person (155).

Thus, instead of being overcome with guilt, there is a sense of 'exalted confidence.' She sees the act for what it is, nothing more and nothing less, "Why did we make such a monstrous thing out of this?" (154).

At their subsequent meeting, there is no awkwardness between them, only a comfortable acceptance of each other. What is radical here is not the fact that Indu has sex outside marriage, but the fact of the absence of guilt. For Deshpande to remove the feminine sexual act from the patriarchal conceptual framework of feminine purity and the imperative of conjugal commitment, in 1983, when the novel was published, was unusual and courageous.

Indu's return to the family and the family house also contributes to her personal journey towards self-knowledge. It's a conversation with Naren which provides a crucial insight:

> Naren's words, satirical, only half-serious were a trigger that suddenly released the truth. I knew in that instant what it was that my life had lacked. It was the quality of courage. I looked back in derision at myself and saw that courage had come to me only in rare moments of blind anger. But that was not enough. What I needed was a steadfastness, and where would I get that? (150).

Indu goes back to her husband Jayant after the family matters are sorted out and Mini has got married. She resolves to build her relationship with him on a more honest basis. "What kind of a life can you build on a foundation of dishonesty, I had asked myself once. What kind of a home have I built? Now I would go back and see if that home could stand the scorching touch of honesty (187). But even as Indu determines to make a fresh start, she is aware of the world that so many women inhabit. A world, confining and monotonous, a prolonged existence in which the mind atrophies.

> To get married, to bear children, to have sons and then grandchildren...they were still for them the only successes a woman could have. I had almost forgotten this breed of women since I had left home. Now, seeing them was like discovering a new world. Each of them, riddled with ignorance, prejudice and superstition, was a world of darkness in herself. And, even more amazing was their ignorance of their own darkness. It was almost superb (116).

In fact, Shankarappa, the man who finally buys the house, refers to this smug complacency:

> ... you people say that we suppress our women. But I tell you...and take it from me, Indu-akka, it's the truth...it's the other way round. How often have I told my wife to change her ideas, to come out of the house, to meet people. Obstinate as donkeys, these women (186).

Deshpande asks a similar question in her essay entitled "Hear Me, Sanjay", when she writes, "have you not seen how different he seems ever since Gandhari uncovered her eyes? He seems at peace with himself, as if an ancient wrong has been righted. She should have done it long back, yes, she should have done this long ago. What use was it blinding herself? Oh, these futile vows! I sometimes think they are just a cover for the wilfullness of self-willed people" (Jain, 2007: 76). What the writer implies is that women often voluntarily put themselves into fetters, just as the Queen Gandhari tied a piece of cloth around her eyes to prevent herself from seeing because her husband was blind. Of course both the story and the question that Deshpande asks work at multiple levels. Thus the true nature of the subjugation of women, the novel indicates, lies not only in society and traditions, but also in their conviction of the validity of their own subjugation. In this context, the efforts at a robust selfhood become especially significant.

(IV)

Women novelists writing in English in India today have come a long way indeed. From the first novel written by Krupabai Satthianadhan in 1894, when she was the solitary voice, to 2010, a hundred and sixteen years have passed. The single voice has grown to a clamour and scores of novels of all hues and themes are being published today. A veritable kaleidoscope of novels is available to the reader of contemporary times. African American novelist Richard Wright, author of the famous novel *Native Son*, while describing the effects of slavery wrote in the first half of the twentieth century, "Scores of years will have to pass before we shall be able to express what this slavery has done to us, for our personalities are still numb from its long shocks; and as the numbness leaves our souls, we shall yet have to feel and give utterance to the full pain we shall inherit" (Wright, 2001: 68). Likewise, the stories of women are also only now beginning to be told. The past fifty years has witnessed an enormous increase in the volume of writings by women in India. The writings are nuanced and address issues about which there was relative silence, for example the questions of autonomy and selfhood. The situation and place of women in society and the importance of acknowledging their contributions to it is a common theme. Gayatri Spivak's famous rhetorical question, "Can the Subaltern peak?" is at least partially answered when the voices of those who are traditionally marginalized and sans voice find expression in these writings.

Note

1. All quotations from the novel *Roots and Shadows* have been taken from Disha Books, an imprint of Orient Longman Limited, 1983 publication.

References

Chakravarti, Uma 1998, *Rewriting History*, (New Delhi : Zubaan).

Deshpande, Shashi 2003, *Writing from the Margin*, (New Delhi : Viking).

Jain, Jasbir 2003, *Gendered Realities, Human Spaces*, (Jaipur: Rawat Publications).

Jain, Jasbir (ed.) 2007, *Growing up as a Woman Writer*, (New Delhi: Sahitya Akademi).

Omvedt, Gail 1995, *Dalit Visions*, (New Delhi : Orient Longman).

Rege, Sharmila (ed.) 2003 *Sociology of Gender* (New Delhi : Sage Publications).

Saxena, Sanjoy 2007, "Women's Identity in Colonial India", *Journal of Women's Studies*, Vol. 1. No. 2.

Tharu, S. & Lalitha, K. (eds.) 1991, *Women Writing in India 600 B.C. to the Early 20th Century*, vol.1 (NewYork: Oxford University Press).

Wright, Richard 2001, "Twelve Million Black Voices" in *Anthology of Modern Prose*, Edited by the Department of English, University of Allahabad.

5

Cosmology, Gender and Kinship: Role and Power Relationships of Himalayan Pastoral Women

Subhadra Mitra Channa

Gender relationships are both complex and multifaceted, informed by multiple forces-social, historical, cosmological and situational. In this chapter, gender relations have been discussed with the help of the ethnography of a Himalayan pastoral community who have been subjected to historical and situational forces over the past few decades that has both led to a change in their social, political and economic conditions and also to multifaceted and nuanced complexities in the interpersonal power relationships of men and women. I problematize the nature vs culture debate as it has been considered by feminist scholars and provide a different perspective on gender relations that exists outside of the Western view of the world. I argue that a different cosmology that looks upon the world in an alternative way also situates men and women differently, giving a different meaning to the relationships and the manner of perception and practice of power and hierarchy. Globalization has the effect of opening up of communities to forces that introduce totalizing perspectives on power and gender relations that make women lose some of the power that may have had in their original cultures and societies. In short, what is considered as modern and progressive may not always bring in more freedom for women. For the community under consideration the persistence of their cosmology and world view has helped to mitigate some of the changes introduced from the outside and helped reinterpret outside influences so as not to affect the actual position of women in any significant way although superficial changes are already visible.

There is a view among anthropologists, both in general (Sacks 1975, Del Valle 1993:15) and more specific to India and South Asia (Sharma 2001:34[1], Hitchcock 1966, Carrin 2007), that the tribal women enjoy greater degrees of freedom than their counterparts in caste society. On the other hand, many western feminist scholars have been supportive of the view that there is an universal subordination of women and that this subordination is rooted in some fundamental characters of human society that are near universal in their occurrence (Wylie1997:33). However, anthropological data from various societies have cast doubt upon this notion of universal domination and also a number of studies have demonstrated the counter currents of women's power. Thus Webster (1975:154) writes, "The recent research of feminist historians and anthropologists helps us identify the variables that relate to women's power in particular cultures and at specific times in history. It reveals that in some cultural contexts and under some conditions women have more power, more prestige, or more influence than originally assumed." Thus what exactly is the women's position in any society can only be ascertained from empirical data and from analysis of the value system, the institutional norms and the cosmological ordering by which the people understand the world around them. It must also be kept in mind that since society is not static and there is a continuos dynamic interaction with the world around, women's position cannot also be viewed in a synchronic manner.

Globalization and the forces of political integration, economic transformation and increased communication networks have led to many transformations in cultures and social relations and the women's position in society cannot remain impervious to such changes. It is also not correct to assume that such changes would always be in the direction of emancipation. In fact, with respect to pre-capitalist societies it has often been demonstrated that with the transformation of the economy and the society by the forces of industrialization and westernization, the position of women has actually deteriorated (Gunewardena and Kingsolver 2007, Gunewardena 2007, Channa 2004). In this chapter I discuss the women's role and decision making as well as their social position among a small group of pastorals in the upper reaches of the Himalayas.

Jad Bhotiyas of Garhwal: Brief History and Ethnography

The Jads are a group that occupy the higher reaches of the Himalayas and derive their identity from the generic category of Bhotiyas (Furer-Haimendorf 1978). They have a pastoral economy based primarily on sheep rearing but keep other animals also and were cross border traders, trading with their *Mitra* partners, the Tibetans on the frontier villages bordering India and Nepal (for more details see Channa 2002, 2005). These people have undergone many changes in their environment, political identity and economy over the past forty years. The major changes in their life began when their economy was disrupted and the political identity reoriented after the Indo–China war in 1962. They were earlier occupying high altitude villages near the Indo-Tibet border and carrying on trade with Tibet. After the war the border was sealed and they were shifted to a lower altitude and the trade activities with Tibet were curtailed. Since then they have undergone many transformations, the most conspicuous being their integration with the Hindu mainland and increasing trade and economic relationships with the people in the lower altitudes. A reorientation of their political identity towards an Indian citizenship is also in the offing. Earlier they would identify themselves as subjects of the Rajah of Tehri. They had little knowledge about the Indian nation and their loyalties were concentrated on the patriarchal figure of their prince rather than in any democratic state. This area was geographically and socially cut off from the Indian mainland by the deep gorges and steep mountains.

The cosmology of the Jads was deeply influenced by the Himalayan mountainous setting to which they felt they belonged and still belong. To them all good life and all that is worth living for is found on the higher altitudes and unsullied nature is pure and sacred. They are fully convinced that their environment is peopled by living gods and sacred beings. To them the plains appear as dangerous and dirty. The men rightfully belong to this world of forests and spirits and they alone can take the sheep to graze in the pastures, from which the women are tabooed. The women are normatively seen as belonging to the world of mundane things and the village is their rightful space.

After the war of 1962, in which India fought with China on the Indo-Tibet border, the army, for its own purpose made roads and built bridges. The motorable roads brought in tourists and the government officials. There was a genuine desire of the state to integrate these people into the mainstream culture. Informants recall that about three decades back, government officials would go from house to house offering jobs to any young man who was even a little educated (women presumably were not asked for as the officials subscribed to the patrilineal values of the mainstream Hindu society). As they move from lower to higher altitudes seasonally the Jad children are given the privilege of shifting from school to school, seasonally. The government has also been putting in money into the village though these have not made much impact except for the bridges and one road that is used by the villagers mostly as a place to sit in the sun. But education and the impact of democracy can be felt in the village. Reservations have ensured that a large number of young men and even women are studying in professional colleges. At the time of my fieldwork, at least four to five men and women were doctors and some ten to fifteen were studying in medical and engineering colleges around the country. One important fact was that there was no relative importance of education for boys. Both boys and girls went to school and college and to study or not to study was an individual decision. In fact, parental control is fairly unknown concept among the Jads.

Men and Women in Jad Cosmology

My entry into the field area in a village of the Jad Bhotiyas of Garhwal was marked by a surprise at the relative dominance of women in all the village affairs. At the time of my study the head of the village panchayat was a woman. Unlike what I had observed in other villages even in Garhwal, the woman in question wielded unquestioned authority. She discharged her duties independently, with no help from any male including her husband. She traveled to the district head quarters all alone. She conducted meetings, took decisions and in short was an effective power holder. She was totally illiterate and had no qualification that marks the 'modern' woman, the kind of women we usually have in mind when we are talking of 'empowerment'. She had seven children, six girls and one boy and her husband was a shepherd. Her elder two daughters had received college education and were married. She lived in the house built by her father as her only brother, being in the army, lived elsewhere.

What made her which she was? I soon found out that she was no different from the general model of Jad women. Among the Jads, a pastoral group, classified under the generic term Bhoityas, women are in charge of the village while the men belong to the wild. The term wild does not have the connotation as it has in Western values system but rather is seen as a pure but dangerous space, the space of the sacred and supernatural beings. The Jad cosmology is an animated world full of living beings, where nature is as alive, animate and interactive as humans. But they make a distinction between what is pure and impure and what is dangerous and what is safe. The village that is constructed in a depression and hidden away from the outside world is regarded as a safe haven from the dangerous world of spirits of the forest, but more importantly of the 'outsiders'. The forests fade away from those near the village that are regularly used by the women to the distant pastures, to be accessed only by the men. One important dimension of Jad cosmology is that, what is unsullied by human contact is the most pure like the high mountain tops, covered in eternal snow, visible from their villages. The house is most impure and the village, the forests are abodes of pure and godly beings, while the pastures are pure, too. The most impure are the plains and the worst in terms of danger and pollution, both real and metaphorical.

Women are impure and men are pure, therefore only men can go where the women cannot, that is to the pastures and the far away mountains (see Channa n.d.).

But the metaphoric devaluation of women that she is impure as compared to men, translates in practical terms to her dominating the economy and social world of the village.

The women do all the work of the village, including agriculture, processing and sale of woolen items that they make. In their traditional division of labour, the women took care of all activities within the village, ritual, social and economic and the men went on long grazing rounds and trading expeditions. Therefore the work of governing the village that is the role of the head of the Gram Panchayat was in the domain of the 'social life' of the village, the Jads saw nothing amiss in a woman assuming power. In fact, even of the other members of the Gram Panchayat, the most vociferous were the women.

Another factor that worked in favour of this particular woman leader was that her husband was a *magpa* husband, something to which we shall return later. Another factor that may be seen as informing the independence of women is the closeness they had with Tibetan culture, because of their long term trade with Tibet and close social interactions. Tibetan women have been described as having greater autonomy and high status compared to other women of South Asia (Diemberger 1993:98).

The World of Women: Kinship and Co-operation

A factor contributing to the enhanced status of women was village endogamy. Women married into households that were just across the street or a stone's throw away. The work groups formed by the women included women of their natal and affinal kin group. Since they are few in number and all concentrated in one place, the cross cutting ties of affinity and consanguinity makes them a close-knit community in the true sense of a primary group. The women born into the community thus do not suffer from a sense of alienation after marriage as is felt by those who are married into distant households by the fact of village exogamy. In fact, one of the reasons for the low status of women in many communities is their alienation from their natal families after marriage. Here the women had no sense of being uprooted after marriage. They lived in close physical and emotional proximity to their own mothers and sisters. One may compare it with the comments made by Susan Harding about women born and married in the same village in Spain (Harding 1975: 303[2]).

The Jads are not however an endogamous community as a whole. Their small numerical strength, in the past, made it a demographic imperative that they take in spouses from other communities. The Jads have thus been habitually marrying into other pastoral communities of Garhwal, namely the Bhotiyas of Niti and Mana, near Joshi Math at Chamoli and the Kinnauires from nearby Himachal Pradesh. They do not, however, marry into the pastoral communities of Kumaoun.

Jad men who do not find a suitable match within the village or who may of choice marry a woman from outside, bring her into the village as a wife. Such wives often have a relatively weaker position as daughters-in- law than those who are born within the village

But Jad women are mobile and the husband cannot prevent his wife from going away to her parent's place if she so wants. But if the natal house of the wife is far away then she might find it both difficult as well as expensive to go very often. Moreover, her position with respect to her own children remains weak as they are born Jads and speak the Jad language and have the Jad identity. I asked a woman who was from Himachal as to whether her children went with her to her parent's house or whether they spoke her language. She said "When they were very young I used to take them with me, but as they are grown up now they do not like to come along. If I speak to them in my language they make fun of me". Her husband quipped in to say, "Well, I married a woman from a far off place so that she could not fight with me and leave for her parent's house as often as she likes". But the opposite is also true, in case of a fight, a woman from another village is more likely to leave her husband and go back to her parents. He would find it more difficult to bring her back than if she were from the same village. Women always like to return to their natal homes and if they are from another place they are always tempted to go back.

Marriage and Residence: The Magpa Husband

Thus the place that a woman holds in a Jad village depends largely on whether she was born there or whether she was born elsewhere. It also made a difference if she was living in her own father's house or in her husband's house. The Jads have a custom much like the Tibetans as discussed by Barbara Aziz (1978), where parents who do not have a son prefer to get a resident son-in-law who moves in with the wife thus reversing the normal practice of virilocal residence. A *magpa* husband, that is, one living in the house of his wife's parents has a low social status. In fact, people both men and women often made fun of such a person and they were regarded as lowly placed on the social scale, not quite a man. It was believed that only a person in really dire circumstances would agree to become a *magpa* husband as they are not looked upon as 'real' men in Jad society. One woman drew her cloth over her face to mimic a *magpa* husband coming into his in-law's place like a daughter–in-law; thus emphasizing the in-between gender role of the incoming son-in-law.

Most *Magpa* husbands were, in fact, those men who belonged to groups outside of the Jad village and had come here in search of a living and resources and the only way in which they could access the common village resources such as pasture land, was by marrying a Jad woman. The Jads follow the same norms as those described by Aziz (1978:126-127) who writes, "The *magpa* marriage is another arrangement by which males are absorbed into the household, a process which shows the priority of residence over paternity in defining the names people carry and perpetrate—Like the adopted, the *magpa* drops his natal house name and uses the affinal house more exclusively". The children belong to the lineage of their mother and more specifically among the Jads, the *magpa* performs the death rituals of his parents-in-law and not of his own biological parents.

A woman born a Jad also has a relative dominance by the very fact of occupying a greater genealogical space in the village of her birth. She has all her agnatic relatives in the village thus both social as well as emotional support. Writing about the Mendes, Cunningham writes, "'Stranger', including spouses who marry into the community, are at a definite disadvantage. In disputes, the party from the outside has little chance of winning, as the villagers will tend to back their 'brother' or 'sister'" (1996: 343). A very similar situation exists in the Jad village as well. For the pastoral Jads, it is the membership of the group that is more important than individual descent. As we have seen the identity is itself spatially constructed. Thus a Jad woman, if she marries within her village, transmits her identity to her child irrespective of who her husband might be.

The most important aspect of their identity is exhibited in the territorial location of the children. Children born in the village are not only considered fully Jad no matter what their parentage may have been, they are also never dislocated. Neither father nor mother will take a child away from the village. Thus there were many children in the village being brought up in the houses of relatives, whose parents may have left the village after divorce or remarriage. One example is that of a man whom I met in my first visit to the village, whose wife was from another village from Kinnaur, and had left him leaving behind a little daughter. Both he and his daughter were living with this man's brother and his family. On a subsequent visit I was told that the man in question had got married again and become a *Magpa* husband to a woman in another village. "What about the daughter?" I asked. "Well, she continues to stay with her father's brother in the village" was the reply. I had not come across a single case where children had been taken away from the village. Even my informants could not recall any in their farthest memory. Thus children were not seen so much as to belong to their father or mother but to the village. Even their upbringing was more of a collective effort than an enterprise centered on the mother. I always found children, including very small infants being carried from lap to lap and being cared for in many different houses. Breast fed babies were also often fed by other women and quite frequently suckled by the grandmothers.

Children of Mothers? Or Children of the Village?

Here we may strongly criticize the western point of view as proposed by Meyer Fortes regarding the 'mother-child' cell as central to the domestic domain and thus refer to the critique built up by feminist scholars (Yanagisako 1987) regarding the universality of the role of the mother and the universal conjunction of the roles of genetrix and nurturer. We may also refer to the eighteenth century Western philosophical equation of women with nature primarily because of her child bearing role and the 'scientific' denigration of women to an inferior intellectual status (Bloch and Bloch 1980). The Jads certainly did not conceive it the 'natural' role of the mother to take care of the infant and to see this dyad of mother and child as the centre of the domestic domain. In fact, I hardly ever saw any mother take care of her own child and would have found it difficult to identify the mothers of most of the babies I knew. Moreover, if a mother got married elsewhere and left her baby behind, people saw it as the most natural thing to do rather than as something 'going against nature'.

Although children are regarded as precious and nurtured with great care, individual women as mothers are not particularly important. Unlike among the strongly patrilineal Hindus, where a woman without a male child may face strong ostracism, no such sentiments regarding motherhood exist among the Jads. There was no case of a woman being subjected to any kind of discrimination because she did not have a son or even a child. This again points to lack of strong lineal sentiments among the Jads. They do not view children as continuities but as valuable assets in the present context. The Jads have little sense of genealogical descent. Filiality rather than lineality is important to them. This is also reflected in the strong position of the daughter in their families. Thus a couple without children may consider themselves unfortunate but it in no way affects the position of the wife in the family. Also parents would never think of depriving a daughter of rights by adopting a son. They always prefer the *magpa* son-in-law, an institution that ensures that the children of the daughter take care of the lineage gods of the grandparents.

Although patrilocality is the norm, actual residence may be adjusted according to the need of the day. Thus although property in the sense of house and land is supposed to pass down to the sons, it may well pass down to the daughter. In fact, in the village some of the most powerful women were those who had inherited their parent's house and property and were having a *magpa* husband.

Property and Inheritance

Patrilineal inheritance of the Jads is also something that is more conceptual than real. While they may say that property passes in the male line, it is only the lineage gods or *kuldevta* that is so passed on. Everything else is passed along in a far more flexible fashion and as we have already discussed, parents always give their entire property to daughters in the absence of sons.

Also since most newly married couples set up their own households, often building the physical structure of the house themselves, it is viewed as the joint property of the couple. Women have their own income and make many items such as woolen sweaters, shawls and other items such as caps and stockings and sell them in the market. Some of them also weave carpets that fetch good price. Since women earn just like the men and many things in the house are bought with her money, these are regarded as her possessions. Thus a widow or even a divorcee may continue to stay in her own house, and in case of remarriage bring the husband into her house rather than moving out herself. A widow has a natural right in this respect and in case of a divorce it remains to be seen as to who has an upper hand. One old woman related to me about the manner in which a divorcing couple fights over every item in the house;

each claiming that it was bought with his or her money. Very rarely does a woman who is born into the village move out of it at marriage. This as we shall presently see is linked to the way marriages are arranged.

Getting Married: Who has the Upper Hand?

Jad women can only marry if a boy asks for their hand in marriage. A similar situation has been noted by Rao (1998:158) for the Bakkarwal pastoral nomads, "Proposals are always sent out by the boy's family, it is for the girl's family to accept or reject. It is said that 'it's the boy's side which goes asking', but it is also said that 'a man takes a woman, and not the other way round'". If we compare the same rule with the Jads, we see that it is not the rule but its location within a wider system of meanings that is important. The more patriarchal Bakkarwals may have interpreted this rule to mean that it is still the men who have an upper hand, but among the Jads it is quite the opposite. Among them the most crucial aspect is not that the men come to ask for the girl in marriage but the fact that the girl or her parents or guardians never say "yes" at the first go. In fact, as they put it, "A man must wear out the sole of his shoes before he can get a girl in marriage". Moreover, all these visits must be accompanied by gifts of '*chang*' (rice beer). When finally a man feels that the girl is ready to say 'yes', he makes her an offer of a nose ring. The acceptance of the nose ring finally announces to the community that a betrothal has taken place. Jokes regarding this painful pursuance by the men are quite common. Once while I was sitting with a group of women, one of them pointed to a woman wearing a rather splendid gold necklace and said, "Look at her, how clever she is? She made her husband give her that (indicating the necklace) before she said 'yes'. Moreover, among them the girl herself has the final say in the matter of her own marriage. If a girl says no, no one else, not even her parents have the authority to even ask her to reconsider. I had met girls well into their thirties, who had been known to have rejected several suitors. Again no matter how old the girl becomes, the parents are not even obliquely supposed to refer to the fact that she is of marriageable age. One must never show any hurry regarding the marriage of a girl. Thus there were quite a few girls in the village who were well above the culturally acceptable marriageable age that is in their late twenties or even into their thirties. But no one ever mentioned this fact and it was totally overlooked in day to day life. Thus the Jad girls hold undisputed agency in matters of their own life and marriage. This trend continues even after marriage, and if a woman wants to walk out on her husband, there is very little he or anyone else can do in the matter. But because the marriage of a Jad girl can never be negotiated, no girl can marry unless a man comes to the village and asks for her in marriage. This greatly reduces, rather makes it impossible for a girl to get married outside the village, unless she runs away with a man from outside. Like the case of a girl who ran away with a Nepali labourer. In most cases the men who come from outside and marry Jad girls, become resident sons-in-law.

Agency and Personhood: A Gendered Evaluation

The Muslim Bakkarwals, studied by Rao (1998), deny agency to the women by virtue of the way personhood is constructed among them, which is strongly linked to a patriarchal ideology, derived from Islam. The women among them are regarded as immature social beings and thus incapable of making important decisions (*phesla*) which can be made only by important men. These men are important by virtue of both age and wealth. Thus the position of women is not simply an outcome of a way of life, for the Bakkarwals are also pastoral and herd sheep and goat like the Jads. It cannot be simply an outcome of the fact that land is not important among them as it is among the agricultural people. Josephide (1985: 10) has importantly linked three variables to show the inferior position of women in the New Guinea society studied by her, "inability of women to own land, together with the practice of virilocality and the ideology of agnatic descent groups, is shown to subordinate women to men".

The Jads show that all three factors can be notionally present but considerably diluted because of the way identity is constructed, as also how the world is cognized. Thus land in itself is not an important factor of either identity or livelihood for what is important to the Jads is access to common resources which is linked to birth and residence in the Jad village, rights to which are equally held by men and women. We may refer to Cunnigham (1996: 338) who write about the Mende of Sierra Leone about the common ownership of village resources, "women form Kpetema (village) have assured access to land, regardless of where their husbands are from, women who marry in have no inherent right to land, and must rely on their husbands to obtain it for them". Although it is considered morally wrong for a girl to conceive before she is married, the child of such a conception is never stigmatized. The child is taken into the mother's lineage and becomes a full fledged Jad with the mother's name. Such a woman would, however, find it difficult to get a husband unless the father of the child marries her. But she has every right to give the child her own lineage identity and no stigma attaches to the child. Thus a Jad woman could independent of a husband bring up a socially accepted child with a Jad identity.

Thus some of the factors that serve to lower the status of women in other societies do not exist among the Jads. Chief among these are practice of village endogan y, the institution of the *'magpa'* husband, the lack of the notion of an illegitimate child, the marginal role of men in the village economy and the central role played by women in kinship. Also there is no pressure on the individual mother to nurture her child. Child rearing is an almost collective activity in which grandparents and other relatives play a major role.

Changes that have been occurring in Jad society has, however, made an imprint on the status of women.

Globalisation and Change

It is not possible to categorize all changes taking place in the Jad village to globalization; for the definition of which we may take as a starting point, Krismundsdattir's (1999: 43) definition, "By globalisation I refer to what people perceive as a shrinking of their world due to such things as new technology in mass communication, the pervasiveness of internet and business interests, the toppling of old regimes and a weakening of long established borders between countries". While for the Jads, television and movies have been a major source of outside influences, there is less impact of other types of technology except that of building of roads. Also, instead of opening of borders, some borders like the Indo-Tibet border that they had been traversing for hundreds of years, were actually closed down. Change for them is more like an exposure to multiple influences such of the Hindus from the plains, the officials of the Indian democracy and also to more advanced form of Buddhism brought in by the lamas who entered this area, after they fled from Tibet. They have been exposed to outsiders, such as Hindu pilgrims and British administrators as well as to local power holders, for long historical periods. But the real change that is coming about is in the formation of a new identity, in the opening up of possibilities that they can be like the people who they earlier considered as far away and belonging to a different world. In the process of integration with wider world of universal religions and global education, they have split themselves into that aspect that still believe in their own cosmology of living gods and animate nature and that part which interacts with city people, reads and writes in the universal languages of English and the national language of Hindi and study and work in cosmopolitan cities.

But when we look at the manner in which change has affected gender relations, not all seems positive. Thus young men who study and get a job in the city, leave behind a young wife who may try hard to look like the girls she sees on television. Since her husband is not a shepherd, she may not engage in the productive activities carried on by women with the wool they get from their men. I have seen such young wives feeling frustrated and useless and taking on Hindu ritual such as fasts and prayers. The opening of this area to Hindu conservative ideas via the media of television and films and also to some extent by face-to-face interaction has brought about some changes in the way people evaluate gender relations. No longer do parents or even young girls favour the *magpa* husband. Girls want to have educated and sophisticated young men as their husbands. They compare the uncouth shepherds with the smart young men they see on the television channels and they desire for such husbands. Since the girls have immense agency in the matter of their own marriage, there is little that the parents can do. Thus not all values have changed equally. Young women remain independent and often make their own decisions about their lives.

Even the parents want educated and job earning sons-in-law. Many expressed a desire to see their sons settled in white collar jobs though some were more disillusioned. Those in favour of sons doing jobs said that the shepherding activities takes the young men away for long periods of time from their homes and they cannot look after their parents. Others were of the opinion that even after education they do not get good jobs and the money earned from shepherding is far greater than the money earned through jobs.

Having imbibed Hindu ideology regarding the role of the mother, many young wives have started emulating the docile role of mainstream Hindu women. They were of the opinion that child rearing is the prime role of the mother. Many young women would spend more time on the children than on productive activities. But at the level of practice this seemed more of an opinion than the reality. Most Jad women were too busy with their various activities to spend too much time with their children but at least they spoke about it as a value.

Widow re-marriage was again neither looked upon as desirable from the normative point of view imposed by Hinduism nor seen as conducive to the welfare of the children. Ideally, it was expected that a mother should stay and look after her children rather that get married again. Educated boys wanted to marry educated girls and they had an ideal in mind of setting up a household that was not like a Jad household at all. It was visualized that the wife would perform household duties and the husband would earn. Except for a very few such households cases were not yet common. A few such married couples were living away from the village, in cities, where they were living most probably like city couples.

The norms of feminine beauty are also changing. The women prefer the large eyed looks of the heroines that they see. Their own 'mongoloid' eyes that are slightly slanting and narrow are looked upon with disfavour.

Although many changes are still imperceptible, yet they are creeping up among them. I saw a distinct change in the personalities of the older women as compared with that of the younger ones. Most of the older women were brash, independent, ate and drank with gusto, would assert themselves in the village and were fun loving and anything but shy. The younger girls appeared grave, were usually shy and less dominating in their behaviour. Some of them were even opting to become Buddhist nuns, an idea inconceivable to the far from ascetic olders Jads.

Thus the ideals that were existing as of today was of 'civilized' men and 'submissive' women as against the 'wild' men and 'dominating' women. There is no doubt that the idea is borrowed from mainstream Hindu society. It is also true that the reality is still far from the ideal. But what is important is that the Jads are now in doubt about their earlier held values. They are looking down on the institutions such as the *magpa.* The more urban and mainstream value of the nuclear family dominated by the bread-earning man, no doubt also imported into India during the colonial times, is becoming a possibility. They have begun to perceive the woman's role as that of mothering. The strength of the women may slowly erode under such pressures. But till such time the Jad women are still ruling over their villages and are the center of social life.

Cosmology Reconsidered

The Jad cosmology where men and women occupy different worlds, with the woman taking care of the social life and the village economy and the men being in the wild or with nature has not changed. As I have discussed elsewhere (Channa, forthcoming), the Jad world view does not separate nature from culture but the habitation from the wild. The wild is not conceived as opposed to civilization but as sacred and pure and men by their superior and ritually pure bodies belong there. The women manage the more mundane and sacred aspects of life associated with the village and human habitation. Unlike in the urban philosophy, where wild is derogatory and civilization is superior, for the Jads the un-spoilt world of nature is superior to all things human for they contain the spirits and gods who according to them exist only in the higher reaches of the mountains where the white snow dazzles their eyes as they look up onto the Himalayas from their village. The women have agency and power in the human habitation but that does not make them superior to the men who have access to the higher reaches of the mountains and the forests and pastures in the upper Himalayas.

Notes

1. B.D. Sharma, in his analysis of introduction of Panchayati Raj in rural India, with its reservation for women notes that in some of the tribal areas there was complete acceptance for such participation from the male leaders," In a recent conference of the traditional heads of Santhals in East Sinhgbhum, it has been unanimously resolved that women should participate in Gram Sabha", similar trends were noticed among the Bhils and Gumla of Jharkhand. (Sharma 2001)
2. "Clearly a woman who was born in the village, who had lived there all her life, who is related by blood to women in other houses, and who is married to a village man related to other village woman is in the strongest of all positions. She has the most sources of inputs and outlets for her voice"

References

Aziz, Barbara Nimri, 1978, *Tibetan Frontier Families*, (New Delhi, Vikas Publications).

Bloch, Maurice and Jean Bloch, 1980, 'Women and the dialectics of Nature in Eighteenth Century French thought' in Carol Mc Cormack and Marilyn Strathern (eds) *Nature, Culture and Gender*, (Cambridge, Cambridge University Press).

Carrin, Marine 2001, 'Women, Adivasis, Subalterns: Perspectives on the empowerment of Santal Women' in Kamal K. Mishra and Janet Huber Lowry (eds) *Recent Studies on Indian Women*, (Jaipur, Rawat Publications), pp. 281-302.

Channa, Subhadra Mitra 2002, ' The Life History of a Jad woman of the Garhwal Himalayas', *European Bulletin of Himalayan Research*, Vol. 22 (Spring) pp. 61-81.

——————————2004, 'Globalization and Modernity in India: A Gendered Critique', *Urban Anthropology* Vol. 33, No. 1, pp. 37-71.

——————————2005, 'The "Descent of the Pandavas": Ritual and Cosmology of the Jad of Garhwal', *European Bulletin of Himalayan Research*, Vol. 28 (Spring), pp. 67-89.

—————————— (forthcoming), 'Wilderness of the Civilization: Knowledge and Perception of the Jad pastoral Community' in Marie Lecomte Tilouine, (ed.) *Nature and Culture in the Himalayas*, (New Delhi, Esha Beteille Publishers), pp. 223-243.

Cuningham, Kiran 1996, 'Let's Go to my Place: Residence, Gender and Power in a Mende Community' in Mary Jo Maynes, Ann Walters, Birgitte Soland and Ulrike Strasser (eds) *Gender, Kinship, Power*, (New York, Routledge).

Del Valle, Teresa 1993, 'Introduction', in Teresa Del Valle (ed.) *Gendered Anthropology*, (London, Routledge), pp. 3-16.

Diemberger, Hildegard 1993, 'Blood, Sperm, Soul and the Mountain: Gender relations, Kinship and Cosmovision among the Khumbo (N.E. Nepal)', in Teresa Del Valle (ed.) *Gendered Anthropology*, (London, Routledge), pp. 88-122.

Furer-Haimendorf, Christop 1978, 'Trans-Himalayan traders in Transition', in James Fischer (ed.) *Himalayan Anthropology*, (Houton, The Hague), pp. 339-357.

Gunewardena, Nandini and Ann Kingsolver 2007, ' Introduction', in Nandini Gunewardena and Ann Kingsolver (eds) *The Gender of Globalization: Women Negotiating Cultural and Economic Marginalization*, (Santa Fe, School for Advanced Research Press), pp. 3-22.

Gunewardena, Nandini 2007, 'Disrupting Subordination and Negotiating Belonging: Women Workers in the Transnational Production Sites of Sri Lanka' in Nandini Gunewardena and Ann Kingsolver (eds) *The Gender of Globalization: Women Negotiating Cultural and Economic Marginalization*, (Santa Fe, School for Advanced Research Press), pp. 35-61.

Kristmundsdottir, Sigridur Duna 1999, ' "Father did not answer that question": Power, Gender and Globalisation in Europe', in Angel Cheater (ed.) *The Anthropology of Power*, (London, Routledge), pp. 42-56.

Harding, Susan 1975, 'Women and Words in a Spanish village', in Rayna Reiter (ed.) *Towards an Anthropology of Women,* (New York and London, Monthly Review Press), pp. 283-305.

Hitchcock, J. 1966, *The Magars of Banyan Hill*, (New York, Holt, Rinehart and Winston).

Josephide, Lisette 1985, *The production of Inequality: Gender and exchange among the Kewa,* (London and New York, Tavistock).

Rao, Aparna 1998, *"Autonomy", Life Cycle, Gender and Status among the Himalayan Pastoralists*, (New York, Berghahn Books).

Sacks, Karen. 1975, 'Engels revisited: Women, the organization of Production and Private Property', in Rayna Reiter (ed.) *Towards an Anthropology of Women,* (New York and London), pp. 211-234.

Sharma, B.D. 2001, 'Women, Panchayats and Rural power Structures' in Ambrose Pinto and Helmut Reifeld (ed.) *Women in Panchayati Raj,* (New Delhi, Indian Social Institute), pp. 25-35.

Webster, Paula 1975, 'Matriarchy; A Vision of Power', in Rayna Reiter (ed.) *Towards and Anthropology of Women*, (New York, Monthly Review Press).

Wylie, Alison 1997, 'Good Science, Bad Science, or Science as Usual: Feminist Critiques of Science', in Lori Hager (ed.) *Women in Human Evolution,* (London, Routledge), pp. 29-55.

Yanagisako, Sylvia 1987, 'Mixed Metaphors: Native and Anthropological models of Gender and Kinship', in Jane Collier and Sylvia Yanagisako (ed.) *Gender and Kinship: Essays towards an Unified Analysis*, (Stanford, Stanford University Press).

6

Creating Intimate Spaces: Women's Marriage Contracts (*Nikahnamas*) Among Indian Muslims

Rehana Ghadially

One of the recommendations of a committee appointed by the government to look into the status of women in India was the reform of Muslim Personal Law. Since then, Muslim women themselves have challenged in civil courts, the archaic nature of family law, appealing to the State to bring about much needed reforms. Embedded in identity politics, Muslim Personal Law has become untouchable. The enactment of a Uniform Civil Code, applicable to women of all faiths, seen as an another pathway to gender equality in marriage and family, has been perceived by many Muslims as an imposition of Hindu Personal Law. This debate has made improving the status of Muslim women in the family a distant one. This chapter examines how in the last decade the impasse has sought to be broken with the attempt at formulation of a standard marriage contract (*nikahnama)* to protect the rights of Muslim women.

Background and Introduction

Since the 1970's there has been considerable debate in India around personal (family) laws-Hindu, Muslim and Christian. A comprehensive report prepared by the Committee on the Status of Women in India (Department of Social Welfare, 1974) stated that while Muslim women have the right to divorce under some conditions, Muslim men enjoy more power as they have the right to unilateral divorce. The committee recommended legislation, as the instrument to bring the Muslim divorce law in line with the needs of society. However, the State so far has failed to legislate on this matter. In October 1983, Shahnaz Shaikh, a twenty-four year old married woman, who now heads a non-governmental organization which assists Muslim women, in matters pertaining to family law, was orally divorced by her husband and was not given the *mehr* (dower) decided upon at the time of marriage. Ms. Shaikh laid the responsibility for her oppression on the State for not enacting gender-just laws (Menon, 1994). In 1985, the Supreme Court granted Shahbanoo, a Muslim woman in her seventies, the right to lifelong maintenance on divorce, under Section 125 of the Criminal Penal Code, which was applicable to all Indian women regardless of their faith. Her husband's appeal to the Supreme Court stated that he was not obliged to pay any further maintenance under the Muslim Personal Law (MPL), as he had paid her the *mehr* (dower) and supported her during the three months of *iddat* that is a three month waiting period before she can re-marry. To improve the status of Muslim women Judge

Chandrachud pushed the State to enact a Uniform Civil Code (UCC)[1] applicable to women of all faiths (Chandrachud, 1987).

The aftermath of Shahbanoo's petition for maintenance has been extensively covered in the Indian media. In brief, the Muslim Personal Law Board (hereafter referred to as the Board)[2], which was formed in December, 1972, to address and protect, among other things, the Muslim Personal Law, mobilized conservative sections of the Muslim community to agitate against the Supreme Court judgment for its interference in the family law of Muslims, for its interpretation of the Koran and tinkering with Muslim identity. They claimed that the *sharia*, on which the family law is based, is divine and immutable and hence their religion was under threat (Engineer, 1987). Embedded in identity politics, reform of Muslim Personal Law or enactment of a Uniform Civil Code has remained problematic[3]. On the other hand, beginning in the 1950s Hindu Family Law has been codified and to some extent reformed[4]. Some parts of the Muslim Personal Law have been codified during colonial rule. The *Shariat* Act of 1937 was the first effort made at codifying Muslim Personal Law[5]. In 1939, the Dissolution of Muslim Marriage Act was passed, which gave women the right to divorce on certain grounds[6].

Despite appeals, the State has maintained a status quo and acted in a regressive way, as evidenced in the enactment of Muslim Women Protection of Rights (on Divorce) Act, 1986[7]. With the passing of this Act destitute divorced Muslim women, like Shahbanoo, would no longer have the right to maintenance sanctioned by Section 125 of the Criminal Procedure Code. The charge leveled against the then ruling Congress Party, for enacting a regressive law, was that it pandered to vote bank politics, reacting to the fear that reform of family law or the enactment of a Uniform Civil Code may mean losing the Muslim. Muslims constitute 13.4% of the population and form almost a quarter of the voters in the states of Kerala and West Bengal and 20% in the state of Uttar Pradesh which provides the single largest block of seats in India's parliament (Mukherjee, 2009). At the other end, to modernize marriage and family law, were a variety of actors who supported either reform of Muslim Personal Law or the enactment of the Uniform Civil Code. Hindu fundamentalist groups and the Bharatiya Janata Party, a national level right-wing political party, support the enactment of a Uniform Civil Code, not so much, it was alleged, to improve the status of Muslim women, but as to bring about a homogenization of Indian society and establish Hindu cultural domination. Indian feminists saw in the Uniform Civil Code the possibility of granting equal rights to all women, including Muslim women. However, they distanced themselves as such a demand has become identified with Hindu communal forces (Agnes, 2009). As reform of Muslim family law has been communalised, left-oriented feminists and women's wings of left-oriented political parties recommended a third alternative, namely, a comprehensive look at all laws — criminal, labor, civil, and personal law to weed out gender bias. By deflecting from an exclusive focus on personal law, the left-oriented feminists saw a better chance of bringing in the much needed reform. Some Indian feminist have advocated the enactment of the Uniform Civil Code and women to be given the choice to opt to have their cases judged, either under their respective personal laws or the Uniform Civil Code

(Kishwar, 1995). Mr. Tahir Mahmood, member of the Law Commission of India, has advocated codification of Muslim Personal Law applicable to all Indian Muslims, regardless of sects, geographical location, etc. This has been opposed by the Board, as it is seen as paving the way for a Uniform Civil Code (Falahi, 2008). At the center of the debate is the question of how Muslim women's rights can be best protected given the communal context and the political and religious reality of the various stakeholders such as the Board, Indian women activists, Muslim women's groups, the State, the *ulema*, Hindu right wing forces, etc.

The politics surrounding reform of Muslim Personal Law or a Uniform Civil Code has led many to assert that the initiative for change is best left to the community. As Muslim Personal Law is considered based on the *sharia* which is divinely ordained, reform according to conservative sections of the community must come from within an Islamic framework. Given the context of contradictory pulls of the conservatives and the progressives both within the Muslim community and the Indian society at large and to keep at bay communal forces from politicising the issue, it has been touted that preparing a model or standard *nikahnama* (marriage contract) which spells out the rights and conditions of the parties involved in marriage, as the safest bet for receiving acceptance from all concerned. The result has been a proliferation of *nikahnamas*; all claiming to uphold the rights of women as spelled out in the *sharia* yet with varied interpretation and each critical of the other. The marriage contract, more commonly referred to as marriage certificate in use in most parts of the country today is formulated by local *kazis* or spiritual heads of various sects, and requires basic information. This includes *mehr* amount, names of the groom and bride, names of the groom and bride's father, two witnesses and a *vakil* (lawyer), the presiding *kazi's* name and their signatures. In addition it has the date, time and place of marriage, and volume and page number of the register kept with the *kazi* is recorded. The Board because of its claims to be representative of all Muslims in India took on itself the task of preparing a model marriage contract which would go beyond the certificate currently in use.

The Model *Nikahnama*

The Board released its model *nikahnama* in May, 2005 at Bhopal. Although the issue of Shah Bano's maintenance sparked the debate for reform, the real bone of contention among Muslim women was the ease with which Muslim men can divorce. The *sharia* gives men the right to divorce provided there has been some effort at reconciliation and the pronouncement is stated three times over three months. Although no figures are forthcoming, there is a popular perception that men recourse to instant divorce or triple *talaq* (*talaq* pronounced three times in one go) more often than necessary. The *sharia* based on the Hanafi law of jurisprudence of which 80% of the Sunni Muslims in India follow, allows *talaq*[8]. The model marriage contract — actually a set of guidelines along which a contract could be designed — of the Board called on the community to avoid the practice of triple *talaq* and use it only in extreme circumstances. It clarified that a divorce without the intervention of a *kazi* was invalid and recommended a series of agents from elders to *ulemas* to act as go-betweens at reconciliation. It recommended part or full *mehr* payment, at the time of marriage and preferably in gold, silver or immovable property, to protect a cash amount from inflation. Two controversial clauses included support for marriage of minors; consent must be obtained from the guardians, if both or either the bride or groom is a minor at the time of marriage and the other was polygamy, if the man treats his wives in a just manner. These guidelines added nothing new and simply reiterated what is in the *sharia*. In early 2007, the Board also recommended the setting up of *sharia* courts in every district for quick disposal of matters relating to personal law and to streamline guidelines for existing *sharia* courts. The Board also recommended that Muslims have recourse to these courts and thus reduce the burden of conventional courts (Unauthored, *Mumbai Mirror*, 2007).

The Muslim community in India is plural in nature composed of a variety of sects with fault lines along class, language, etc. Disenchanted with the work of the Sunni sect dominated Board and skepticism as to whether it had any religious authority, the Ithna Ashari Shias[9], the Barelvi Sunni sub-sect[10] and some Muslim women's organizations, decided to form their separate personal law boards. The Shias who constitute about 1.09% of the Indian population and 10–15% of the Muslim population in India (http://en.wikipedia.org/wiki/Shia_ Islam# Demographics) challenged whether the Board is the sole representative of all Muslims and set up the All India Muslim Shia (Ithna Ashari) Law Board (here after referred to as the Shia Board). Many sects practice their own brand of personal law representing a mixture of customary practices, the particular school of jurisprudence such as Hanafi, Maliki and Shafi, Ismaili; and their interpretation of the *sharia*. The Barelvi sect threatened to protest and draw up their *nikahnama*, if the Board banned triple *talaq*, and Muslim women's groups felt that the model marriage contract had failed to protect women's rights, granted under the *sharia*. In defense of the Board, it did consider their model marriage contract as optional and subject to change.

The fundamental disagreement of Muslim women's groups to the model *nikahnama* is that it fails to safeguard the rights of women. More specifically it centers on the fact that it does not ban triple *talaq*, does not spell out women's right to divorce; and by insisting on *sharia* courts to settle marital disputes, the Board precludes women's right to approach secular courts. Besides, the Board's model *nikahnama* does not recommend compulsory registration of marriage and for the dower to be paid in full to the bride on the day of marriage. It also fails to regulate polygamy and is silent on the minimum age of marriage of Muslim girls.

Sectarian and Women's *Nikahnamas*

As the Board capitulated to the demands of the Barelvi sect and inserted the guideline to avoid triple *talaq* rather than ban it, the Barelvi Board's marriage contract is yet to see the light of day. The Shia Board formed in January 2006, released its marriage contract at Lucknow in May 2006. It tried to some extent to address women's rights. It clarifies that dowry is un-Islamic and condemns triple *talaq*. It gives both men and women the right to initiate divorce with community arbitration. It recognises women's right to separate living if there is harassment in the marital home. If the husband divorces her, she retains the right to *mehr* and the husband has to guarantee a monthly maintenance to the divorced wife until such time that she is able to gain her own source of livelihood. Besides, the groom must declare his income and his education at the time of marriage so the bride and her family may avoid being duped (Times News Network, 2006). The claim of the Shia Board is that their marriage contract is already in use.

Even before the Board's model marriage contract saw the light of day, the initiative to write up a *nikahnama* was in fact first taken by women. It was seen as one of the principal means by which the unprotected rights of women and customary practices disfavoring women could be addressed. As Islamic feminism has been the preferred framework to address women's rights in marriage and family in Muslim majority countries (Mirza, 2008), Muslim women in India have also adopted a feminist position within an Islamic framework as the best way to set things rolling. In the city of Mumbai, as early as 1994, a group of mostly women academicians, lawyers and religious scholars, prepared a marriage contract centered on divorce. It stipulated that both parties nominate a person to arbitrate for reconciliation for a three month period. If the husband violates the marriage contract and pronounces *talaq* three times in one sitting, he would have to pay his wife double the *mehr*. The group recommended insertion of *Talaq-e-Tawfid* clause, wherein a man delegates his right to divorce to his wife if the husband brings in a second wife without the consent of the first[11]. Niloufer Akhtar — a Mumbai based lawyer who worked closely with the Board proposed a model marriage contract along similar lines as the above mentioned group with one exception. She expanded the contingencies under the *Talaq-e-Tawfid* clause to include a wife's right to divorce if the husband is HIV positive and conditions similar to those stated in the

Muslim Marriage Dissolution Act, 1939 (Katakam, 2004). In the mid 1990's, the documents were presented and considered by members of the Board at their Mumbai meeting but were set aside.

Grounded in personal and/or local experiences, other Muslim women's groups in various parts of India formulated marriage contracts, as alternatives to the Board's model contract. Towards the end of 2005, as an immediate reaction to the release of the model marriage contract, the *Muslim Women's Rights Network* in Mumbai and *Shaheen* a social organization in Hyderabad drafted their *nikahnamas*. In Lucknow, Shiasta Ambar formed the All India Muslim Women's Personal law Board (hereafter referred to as Women's Board) and with the help of thirty members the advisory committee formulated and released its document in March 2008, variously labeled as the "*sharia*", "women friendly", "parallel" and "revolutionary" *nikahnama*. This is a comprehensive twelve pages document of which four constitute the actual contract and the rest contain 17 guidelines for marriage under the *sharia* law. It also includes an eight point action plan on the process of *talaq*. The document is applicable to both Sunni and Shia sects and is written in Hindi and Urdu languages to make it accessible to more women.

The three issues highlighted in the *nikahnama* prepared by the Women's Board which is similar to what the *nikahnamas* prepared by other Muslim women's groups, include divorce, the rights of women and compulsory registration of marriage[12]. The guidelines bans triple *talaq* and makes completion of three menstrual cycles a must during which a woman must stay in her marital home for the divorce to be considered valid. The guidelines further state that if men declare *talaq* in a state of anger, intoxication or partial sleep; the divorce would not be considered valid. As the new information and communication technologies have added to the ease, divorce over telephone, email, SMS, internet, video and newspaper is invalid and so is divorce given to a pregnant wife. Under the *talaq*, all the gifts received during the wedding and after would be the bride's property. The document also spells out the grounds on which a wife could initiate divorce. These are similar to those covered in The Dissolution of Muslim Marriages Act, 1939, with some new additions[13]. If the husband's consent to divorce is not forthcoming, the woman has the right of separation by returning the *mehr*. Besides, granting women the right to separation and divorce, it prescribes her right to maintenance, to a home free of violence and dowry considerations.

Making registration of marriages compulsory for all Indians irrespective of religion has been a hotly debated issue and women activists of all hues have strongly urged the government to act in this matter.[14] In Muslim law, a marriage is regarded as a civil contract and the *kazi* or officiating cleric, also records the terms of the marriage in a *nikahnama*, which is handed over to the married couple. In India, a marriage contracted through a religious ceremony is valid even if not registered. Registration of marriages serves two important purposes; one is proof of marriage and recording the requisites to marriage, especially age of groom and bride at marriage. Insight from other Muslim countries show that the legislation of compulsory registration ensures state's desire to protect women's rights in marriage and/or the state's desire to reduce the social power of the clerics (International Solidarity Network, 2003). The women activists preparing the contracts ought to argue not just for the registration of marriage but also registration of marriage contracts. The Women's Board *nikahnama* recommends the compulsory registration of marriage with government officials. According to the Women's Board it is meant to protect women from unscrupulous men, especially non-resident Indians and Arabs, who give the temporary union a religious touch without any documentary proof of marriage. Registration safeguards women who find it difficult to prove their marriage when deserted, especially when they or their natal families wish to have recourse to civil courts. Presumably, compulsory registration will make marriage of minors and polygamous unions difficult, on which the Women's Board guideline is silent. The core issues similar across the women's *nikahnamas* pertain to curtailing men's right to unilateral divorce and expanding the conditions for and facilitating women's right to divorce. All Muslim women's groups agree on banning the triple *talaq*, but disagree on the nature of punishment for the erring husband — whether to levy a monetary fine, pay double the amount of *mehr*, raise the amount of *mehr* to ten times that of the amount fixed at the time of marriage or make the triple *talaq* revocable. Regarding *talaq-e-tafwid*, some want women to have an absolute right to delegated divorce, others want it to be related to polygamy; whereas still others stipulate a wider set of conditions, under which a woman can divorce without the husband's consent. The difference among the women's groups and independent Muslim scholars on the other hand center on polygamy — some want to ban it, some want to regulate it, some are silent on it.

Reactions to the Women's Marriage Contracts

The reactions to the women's *nikahnamas* have been mixed, limited to an elite section of the society either individual or group, and receiving part or overall support for the documents. The Board and the Shia Board have dismissed women's marriage contracts, the former claiming it as unnecessary, an exercise in semantics, and with claims that its model *nikahnama* protects women's rights better. Begum Naseem Iqtedar Ali, the only woman on the executive committee of the Board dismissed the new *nikahnamas* stating that these detract the community from core issues such as poverty, lack of education and under-representation in government jobs (Ramakrishnan, 2008). The Shia Board claims that the women's *nikahnamas* are similar to their own. The members doubt legal sanctity of the women's contracts and claim that these encourage marital breakdown. Some clerics have also rejected the women's marriage contracts as redundant, a publicity stunt and requiring undue paperwork and called it a *jihadi nikahnama* (Ramakrishnan, 2008; Mishra, 2008; Gidwani, 2008). A member of the Board labeled the marriage contract as useless and irrelevant (The Hindu, 2008). By an outright dismissal, rather than a balanced critique, both Boards —Sunni and Shia and independent clerics have closed the democratic process of involving women in aspects close to their lives and the doors to debate and dialogue vital to the improvement of women's condition. Women Muslim or otherwise, with left-oriented politics are willing to settle for nothing less than complete equality. Some independent observers have dismissed it as only a good beginning.

Many observers including some liberal clerics view the women's *nikahnamas* as many shades better in advancing the cause of women than the Board's model marriage contract. Tahir Mohammad, an Islamic law expert and member of the Law Commission of India stated that the main propositions conform to the *sharia* in letter and spirit and are in accord with the codes of Muslim law in major Muslim countries (Ramakrishnana, 2008). Progressive, secular and left non-governmental Muslim organizations have condemned triple *talaq* and asked for its legal ban (Times News Network, 2004). They would favor a clause that does away with men's unilateral right to instant divorce. While dissatisfied with the notion of using a marriage contract to protect women's rights in marriage and family, some members of the Muslim community are willing to concede that a beginning has been made and things can now move further in the right direction. By and large the voices of ordinary Muslim women remain mute and unexamined on the matter.

Muslim World Scenario: Insights and Lessons

Formulating a Uniform Civil Code, reform of Muslim Personal Law and drafting a standard marriage contract have been debated and discussed as the appropriate means to offer relief and justice to the Indian Muslim women. In the contemporary debate, a pre-nuptial agreement has been accepted as the best of the rest in offering both gender justice and at the same time satisfying some of the stake holders in the debate and keeping other stakeholders at bay for the present moment. The marriage contract is very much a part of an Islamic framework, true of all schools of jurisprudence whether Sunni or Shia. Its nature and content maybe be open to debate but as a tool to spell out the rights and obligations of both spouses and as an instrument to protect women from arbitrary and archaic customary practices cannot be challenged. In this context it is pertinent to examine in brief the role of marriage contracts and passing of gender fair family laws in select Muslim communities around the world in meeting this challenge. The International Solidarity Network in their worldwide survey of women, family law and customs published in 2003 noted that countries could be classified according to laws related to negotiated rights and responsibilities in marriage. The more option-giving laws are those laws which clearly state the possibility of rights and responsibilities and secondly facilitate negotiations by having marriage contracts/registration forms that clearly provide for specified and/or additional negotiated clauses. Pakistan, Bangladesh, Iran and Malaysia fall into this category. In Pakistan and Bangladesh, the standard marriage contract under the *Rules of the Muslim Family Law Ordinance* carries provision for *talaq-e-tafwid* and restrictions on the husband's right of divorce. Besides, there is no restriction on including any additional conditions provided there is mutual agreement between the two parties.

The middle ground, in terms of option-giving laws, are those that explicitly recognise the possibility of negotiating terms and conditions to the marriage contract but do not facilitate negotiation through standard marriage contracts/registrations forms. These include Morocco, Algeria, Sudan, Tunisia, Egypt, Cameroon, Indonesia and Turkey. In the Maghreb (Morocco, Algeria, Tunisia), progressive family laws have been passed since the survey. For example, in January 2004, the government of Morocco adopted a new landmark family law supporting women's equality and granting them new rights in marriage and divorce, among others (Women's Learning Partnership, 2004). Historically, the role of *sharia* in Tunisian law has been marginalised (Voorhoeve, 2008). Between 2000 and 2004, Egypt similarly introduced three new family laws favorable to women — to travel internationally without the husband's written approval, file for a no-fault divorce, right to file for divorce from unregistered marriages and establish a family insurance fund through which female litigants could collect court-ordered alimony and child support (Batrawy, 2008). Turkey has abandoned the *Turkish Civil Code* and replaced it with a *New Civil Code* which defines the family as a union based on equal partnership. The middle ground in terms of option giving laws is also occupied by those countries which have an un-codified law and no standard marriage contract, but negotiated conditions are recognised. India, Nigeria and Saudi Arabia fall into this category. As mentioned earlier, there is as yet no standard marriage contract in India for those marrying under Muslim law. However, informal adjudication forums such as community or mosque committees, as well as case law in the civil courts, recognise valid conditions to a Muslim marriage contract (International Solidarity Network, 2003).

The lower middle ground is occupied by laws which are silent about the possibility of negotiating conditions; or do not see marriage as a negotiable contract but recognise 'nuptial agreements'. In Sri Lanka, the Muslim Marriage and Divorce Act, 1951 does not mention about the possibility of negotiating conditions. The marriage register does not provide space for recording negotiated conditions or additional documents. The law in Fiji, South Africa and Turkey does not view marriage as a contract. In Turkey, the only pre-nuptial agreement possible is a choice among three options for marital property settlement. The least option-giving are those laws which explicitly prohibit additional agreement to a marriage. The Central Asian Republics fall in this category.

Has the passing of progressive laws or having a standard marriage contract with safeguards included empowered women? The results are mixed and in general show limited benefits for women. For example, despite gender just laws women activists in the Maghreb have found that women are ignorant of the new rights granted by law or cannot comprehend them (Arfaoui, 2009). Besides, lack of education among women and the corruption of the justice system can undo the best laws (Erlanger and Mekhennet, 2009). In Egypt, a study published in 2008 found that women are not aware of what the new laws mean and how to access the justice system. Besides, the implementation of new laws continue to reflect gender bias (Batrawy, 2008). Standard marriage contracts on the other hand pose a different set of problems. Women consider the right to add certain demands in a marriage contract as inappropriate, and believe that such a daring step may reduce their chances in marriage (Arfaoui, 2009; Batrawy, 2008). The experience in Pakistan shows that usually the optional clauses in a marriage contract are struck out, especially *talaq-e-tafwid* (International Solidarity Network, 2003).

Despite progressive family laws, for several reasons, women activists in the Maghreo countries have felt the need and prepared a standard marriage contract which if certified will better protect women's rights. A contract that is simple and clear in language and which incorporates the conditions granted by law will not only protect them better but also enable women to get acquainted with the existing legislation. The activists argue that progressive laws or marriage contract may take women only part of the way; what is needed is favourable social and institutional conditions and a supportive political and cultural environment if laws and contracts are to protect women's rights. There is also agreement among activists that what is needed in reform efforts is dialogue among NGOs, Islamic scholars, legislators, families coupled with a need to put greater focus on educating the next generation on equality, justice and respect (Batrawy, 2008).

Near Yet So Far Away

Coming back to India, what is one to make of the number of marriage contracts produced, all ostensibly claiming to be within the boundaries of the *sharia* and protecting women's rights and the debates and discourse surrounding them? There are benefits and limitations of such an approach to dealing with what is a difficult and sensitive issue. Firstly, looking at the situation from a positive frame, since all schools of Islamic law (Sunni or Shia) recognise contractual freedom of the groom and bride and once they are signatories to such a document, the two parties are bound by it, this constitutes a good beginning. Secondly, the different Boards and Muslim women's groups by providing guidelines and model contracts may encourage some women to go beyond the bare information in structured contracts in use today. Thirdly, if the bride chooses to exercise the right to a marriage contract, her privileges can be enhanced significantly, going beyond divorce, *mehr* and maintenance, by inserting her right to pocket money, mobility for education and work and property settlement. Fourthly, the new millennium also marks a beginning of Indian Muslim women's aggressive engagement with issues that touch their lives in intimate ways and the courage to defy and resist traditional authority whether religious or secular. Lastly, the media coverage of *nikahnama*, as an instrument to protect women's rights may serve to popularise the notion that Muslim women have the right to set conditions before marriage and that the *sharia* is open to a variety of interpretations. The proliferation of marriage contracts has also challenged a monolithic view of the community and brought to the fore the diversity of Muslims and the different shades of personal law each sect follows.

The marriage contract as an approach to enhance women's privileges has its drawbacks. Firstly, while men have followed the debate in the papers women are pretty much ignorant about it (Ramakrishnan, 2008); hence the majority of ordinary Muslim women may still have to wait long before the benefits from any progressive change reaches them. Secondly, a woman is in a position to set conditions before marriage if she is empowered with education, has a supportive family and a sympathetic *kazi* who oversees the *nikah* (marriage ceremony). Secular education and skills necessary for economic sustenance are two vital tools of empowerment. According to the Sachar Committee Report, (2006), chaired by Justice Sachar, the majority of Muslim women in India lack both of these. Hence, a gender sensitive *nikahnama* may be a deceptive gain. According to Flavia Agnes, who runs a legal advocacy program for women in Mumbai, a marriage contract is a personal document not binding in a court of law. She advocates that Muslim women move the civil courts to seek justice (Agnes, 2009). Thirdly, finding a solution in a marriage contract to address the grievances of women has postponed the need for codification and reform of Muslim Personal Law or the possibility of a Uniform Civil Code which offers an opportunity for all Indian women to bond together. Fourthly, sections of the Muslim community with a secularist hue contest the notion that Islam is the only model within which women's rights can be addressed. In the Egyptian context, Abu-Odeh argues that sacrifice of secular space for reform that are couched purely in religious terms may be problematic as they may prove hard to critique after a while (quoted from Mirza, Q. 2008). Besides, how the drawing up of several *nikahnamas* will affect the material reality of women's lives remains to be seen. Finally, as long as the gender rights debate remains within a religious framework, the various interpretations of the *sharia* may bring some improvement, but whether it can bring equality for women remains an open question. Ghosh (2009) argues that where family laws are concerned, the Indian judiciary has made progressive pronouncements and that these reforming outcomes will enter into official law as case law and then people will gradually become habituated to the new laws.

Notes

1. The Constitution of India 1950, Article 44 reads, "The State shall endeavour to secure for the citizens a uniform civil code throughout the territory of India". However, it was stated among the list of DirectivePrinciples of State Policy rather than among the Fundamental Rights, thus making it non-binding on the State to enact a UCC applicable to women of all communities ("Nobody can direct House on uniform civil code : SC" Times News Network. The Times of India 20 Oct 2008).

2. The All India Muslim Personal Law Board has a working committee of forty one *ulemas* representing various schools of thought. In addition to this, it has a general body of 201 persons of ulemas as well as laymen including 25 women. Within the Board, the Deobandi sect of Sunnis dominate and the Shia branch of Islam and the Barelvi sect of the Sunnis are in a minority (for the composition of the Board. (from http://en.wikipedia.org/wike/All_India_Personal_Law_Board (accessed on 23 Sept, 2009).
3. For details on inter-communal politics of personal law debates in India see Partha S. Ghosh "Politics of Personal Law in India: The Hindu-Muslim Dichotomy" *South Asia Research* 2009,29 (1) 1-17.
4. In the mid 1950s under the leadership of Ambedkar and the congress party Prime Minister P. J. Nehru, the Hindu Code was reformed in a gradual but limited manner so as to not alienate the conservative and pro-Hindu leaders of the Congress party.
5. The Shariat Act of 1937 is applicable in matters such as: interstate succession, property of females, marriages, dissolution of marriage, maintenance, dower, guardianship, gifts, trust and trust properties, wakfs. According to the Shariat Act 1937, a husband has an absolute right to repudiate the marriage. However, the wife has the right to ask for divorce by *khula* or *mubarat* that is divorce by mutual consent. In both these cases the wife loses her right over her *mehr*. (Geetanjali Gangoli: The Discourse around Muslim Personal law: 1947-1996. *Women Law and Customary Practices.* Special Paper Commissioned by Women's Research and Action Group. Mumbai, 1997).
6. In1939, the Dissolution of Muslim Marriage Act was passed, which attempted to give the Muslim women the right to divorce under certain grounds: such as if the husband is missing for more than 4 years, if the husband has neglected or failed to maintain the wife for 2 years, if the husband has been imprisoned for 7 years or more, if the husband is impotent at the time of marriage and continues to be so, if husband treats her with

cruelty. In addition, the Act gives women the right to repudiate a marriage at puberty, if she is married before she was fifteen years old, provided the marriage is not consummated (Gangoli, 1997). To have recourse to this law one has to move the civil court which most Muslim women do not, preferring instead the arbitration by a *kazi*.

7. The Act allows for a reasonable provision paid to her within the period of the *iddat*, a provision for maintenance of children for 2 years, the dower agreed at the time of marriage, all properties given to her by her husband and natal family. (Sen, K. A. 1987 'The Muslim Women (Protection on Rights on Divorce) Bill, 1986',in Engineer, A. A. (ed.) (1987 : pp 85-88.) The Act perceived as regressive, the judiciary, however, has legislated in a progressive manner.

8. The issue of triple *talaq* has been a contentious one in India. According to some, Hanafi law approves it, others consider it un-Islamic, some contend that it is valid in extreme circumstances and still others maintain that it is valid only if the woman is desirous of an immediate divorce.

9. The Shia community in India is divided into two main branches: the Ithna Asharis or Twelver Shias and the Ismailis. The latter are sub-divided into two sub-sects namely the Aga Khanis and the Dawoodi Bohras. Each follows its version of the *sharia* known as Ismaili law.

10. Two-thirds of India's Sunni Muslim subscribe to the Barelvi School (http://en.wikipidia.org/wki/Islam_in_India (accessed on 3rd Oct; 09).

11. In systems based on Muslim laws, *talaq-e tawfid* entails a husband delegating his unilateral right to divorce to his wife. This agreement can be made through the marriage contract or it can be negotiated subsequently. The delegation of right may be absolute or conditional. In India, there is a long tradition of *talaq-e-tawfid* and there is a wealth of case law. (Knowing Our Rights: Women, family, laws and customs in the Muslim world.

International Solidarity Network. Zubaan (an imprint of Kali for Women) Delhi, 2006.

12. In India, there is no code that requires marriage registration. However, some communities, recognise the benefit of keeping a public record of marriage documents. In Bengal, official procedures exist for voluntary centralised registration of Muslim marriages. In other communities, a copy of the marriage certificate may be kept with the local mosque or community council (from International Solidarity Network, 2003, "Knowing our Rights: Women, Family, Laws and Customs in the Muslim World", Women living Under Muslim Law, London).
13. The AIMWPLB spells out the ground on which divorce could be initiated by the wife. These include extra-marital relationship, absence of physical relationship between the husband and wife for more than a year, abandonment of the wife for more than four years, failure of the husband to look after the wife and the family or any kind of ill treatment or torture, incompatibility and not disclosing that he is an AIDS patient at the time of marriage or contracts it after marriage. If the husband refuses divorce she has the right to separation.
14. The government of India while agreeing in principle to the idea of compulsory registration of marriage, has found the task impractical in practice.

References

Agnes, F. 2009, 'India: Flavia Agnes on Muslim Personal Law Reforms'. Retrieved September 23, 2009, from http://www.awid.org/eng/Issues-and-Analysis/Library/India-Flavia-Agnes-on-Muslim-Personal-Law-Reforms/%28language%29/eng-GB.

Arfaoui, J. 2009, 'Maghreb Activists Propose New Marriage Contract to Protect Women'. Retrieved January, 31, 2010 from http://www:magharebia.com/cocoon/awi/xhtml1/en_GB/features/awi/features/2009/04/15/feature-01.

Batrawy, A. 2008, 'New Family Laws: Success Story?' Retrieved January, 29, 2010, from http://ipsnews.net/news.asp?idnews=44281,

Chandrachud, C. J. 1987, 'In the Supreme Court of India: Criminal Appellate Jurisdiction', In Engineer, A. A. (ed.), 1987, *The Shah Bano Controversy* (Hyderabad :Orient Longman Limited), pp. 23-34.

Engineer, A. A. 1987, 'Introduction', In Engineer , A. A. (ed.), 1987, *The Shah Bano Controversy*. Orient Longman Limited. Hyderabad. pp. 1-19.

Engineer, A. A. 1987, 'S. C. Judgment on Maintenance: Forces behind the Agitation', In Engineer, A. A. (ed.) *The Shah Bano Controversy*. Orient Longman Limited. Hyderabad. pp. 35-41.

Erlanger, S. & Mekhennet, S. 2009, 'Family Code gets Nudge, but Women seek a Push'. *The New York Times*. Retrieved January 31, 2010, from http://www.nytimes.com/2009/08/19/world/africa/19tangiers.html?_r=1&pagewanted

Fal-ahi, A. M. 2008, 'Need For Modification of Shariat Act 1937, Codification of Islamic Law for all Muslims in India' (Interview with Tahir Mahmood, Member of Law Commission of India). Retrieved November, 26, 2009 from http://www.twocircles.net/2008jul26/need_modification_shariat_act_1937_codification_islamic_law_all_ muslims_ india.html.

Gangoli, G. 1997, 'The Discourse around Muslim Personal Law: 1947-1996', from *'Women, Law and Customary Practices'* Special Paper Commissioned by Women's Research and Action Group (WRAG) Mumbai.

Ghosh, S. P. 2009, 'Politics of Personal Law in India: The Hindu-Muslim Dichotomy', *South Asia Research*, vol. 29, no. 1, pp. 2-18.

Gidwani, D. 2008, 'New Nikahnama Sparks Controversy'. March 17th. g.deepak@naindia.net.

Government of India (Sachar Committee), 2006, *'Social, Economic and Educational Status of the Muslim Community of India: A Report'*. Delhi: Prime Minister's Office'.

Government of India, 1974, '*Towards Equality: Report of the Committee on the Status of Women*'. Delhi: Ministry of Education and Social Welfare. Department of Social Welfare.

Katakam, A. 2004, 'The Divorce Debate', *Frontline,* Vol. 24, no. 18. Retrieved August 28, 2009 from, http://www.hinduonnet.com/fline/fl2118/stories/2004091 000230 4100.htm.

Kishwar, M. 1995, 'Stimulating Reform, not Forcing it: Uniform versus Optional Civil Code', *Manushi,* vol.89, July-August, pp. 5-14.

Menon, R. 1994, 'The personal and the political: an interview – discussion with Shehnaaz Sheikh, In Bhasin, K., Menon, R., & Khan, N. S., (eds), 1994, '*Against all Odds: Essays on Women, Religion and Development from India and Pakistan*'. Kali for Women. New Delhi.

Mirza, Q. 2008, 'Islamic Feminism and Gender Equality', *ISIM Review,* Vol. 21, pp. 30-31.

Mishra, M. 2008, 'Women Friendly Nikahnama Out', *The Times of India*, March 18, 2008.

Mukherjee, K. 2009, 'All Bets off on India's Crucial Muslim Vote'. Retrieved September 16, 2009, from http://www.reuters.com/article/latest crisis/iduSDEL 355244.

Ramakrishnan, V. 2008, 'Personal Law: Women's Charter'. *Frontline.* Vol. 25, No. 7.

Unauthored, 2004, 'Activists Flay Verbal 'Talaq' Seek Ban'. *Times News Network* 2nd September. Retrieved January 4, 2008, from http://www.mfsd.org/puneemeet.htm.

Unauthored, 2006, 'Model Nikahnama: Women's Group are Skeptical'. *Times News Network, Times of India,* 27th November.

Unauthored, 2007, 'Now, Shariat Courts in Every Districts. *Mumbai Mirror*, 7th February, 2007.

Unauthored, 2008, 'Muslim Women Personal Law Board Unveils New 'Nikahnama". *The Hindu.* Retrieved November 29, 2009, from http://thehindu.com/2008/03/17/stories/2008031759 171700.htm

Voorhoeve, M. 2008, 'Sharia and National Law in Tunisia' Paper presented at the *Annual Meeting of the The Law and Society*

Association, Hilton Bonaventure, Montreal, Quebec, Canada, Retrieved January, 29, 2010, from http://www.allacademic.com/meta/p236212_index.html.

Women's Learning Partnership for Rights, Development and Peace, 2004, 'Morocco Adopts Landmark Family Law Supporting Women's Equality'. Retrieved January, 29, 2010 from http://www.learning partnership.org/advocacy/alerts/morocco0204.

7

Epistemology, Pedagogy and Politics of Women's Studies

U. Kalpagam

Epistemology refers to ways of knowing and ways of producing knowledge. Is there a specific and unique epistemology for women's studies? This requires us first to understand what is 'Women's Studies' ? Here I think there are many ways of understanding what it is. Surely it deals with women and that is probably what would be common to the different ways of understanding it. In recent years there was an attempt by a group of academics and intellectuals within the University Grants Commission in India to rename Women's Studies centres as 'Family Studies' and needless to say there was a group of women that opposed to it. What does this difference of opinion signify? Those supporting 'Family Studies' felt that women's roles in the family were unique and of singular importance, and that women cannot be pulled out of the family context and studied in isolation as if the family did not exist or did not matter. They also felt that 'Women's Studies' was identified too closely with feminism, a notion that they did not accept and could not identify with.

'Family Studies' proponents have a penchant for foregrounding the feminine principle both in the family and in the culture at large and they understand the feminine principle in terms of creativity and reproduction, the life-giving powers that animates the earth. Thus they often invoke the high status accorded to women in Hindu scriptural and mythological literature where the representation of Hindu goddesses are so varied in their powers, emotions and comportment as if to portray the variegated identities and roles of women in society. Such assessment of the superior status of women in Hindu culture is not only admirable but is certainly important for a cognitive understanding of how culture and emotion guide attitude, behaviour and action by and towards women. However an uncritical acceptance of this stance have led to essentialised notions of culture that feed into a kind of cultural politics in contemporary times that is inimical to the freedom cherished by modern women. It is also important to take note of the actual status and condition of women that is grossly at variance with the idealised notions of women.

Those opposing 'Family Studies' noted that the family while being crucial to all women is not the only site of women's activities as many women have roles and responsibilities outside the sphere of the family such as work and community and social roles. Secondly, they tended to think that those espousing 'Family Studies' had an idealistic conception of the family, a romanticised image of the family as the site of love, care and nurturance and that the actualities of family experience may vary from the idealised norm. More specifically, they were of the view that the family itself was a site of women's oppression with patriarchal power subjugating them and that both the feminine mystique and the mystification of the family needed to be unpacked. Also in their view, 'Women's Studies' had to aspire to change and transform women's lives, helping them tours individually and collectively negotiate both patriarchal and other social power relations that enmesh their lives and to that extent it was indeed a feminist agenda, howsoever feminism may be defined.

I have chosen to highlight this debate because it immediately sets the question-where do we start from? Do we start our analysis from the family or from the women? Epistemologically, starting from the family would take us down the trajectory of home economics and family welfare, of how women's family roles could be supported to ensure family well-being. This is no doubt important but it limits the perspective to women's primary role as home-maker whereas women of all ages, classes, castes, religion, ethnic groups, nationalities are discriminated in various other social, public and economic realms as well. If we are to be able to cognise the whole range of social, economic, political and cultural inequalities, deprivation, discrimination, humiliation, and silencing of women's "voices" in myriad circumstances, then clearly the family would be an inadequate starting point and we have to start our cognitive exercise from the position of women. If we start from the position of women, then it is possible to encompass the whole range of family- related issues that affect family well being as well, for after all women are everywhere and in different ways home-makers, nurturers and care givers, and play crucial reproductive, productive and cultural roles in the family.

Women's life experiences are the fundamentals for understanding women's position. But from 'experience' it is necessary to traverse an epistemological terrain to grasp social structures and social relations within which experience occurs and is embedded. If we start from the position of women, then we have to realize that each woman's experiences may vary individually and may also have commonalities across all women or groups of women within each society and culture. The issue now is - how do we cognise women's experience? One way is to let women speak and to narrate their experiences. This also raises issues of whether all experiences could be articulated and comprehended. Take for instance mental pain that cannot perhaps be fully articulated and comprehended. There are also limits placed by cultural norms of what can and cannot be said. The French sociologist Bourdieu has given a theoretical exposition of this phenomenon in terms of 'habitus' and 'doxa' that explains culturally proscribed discourses that individuals abide by (Bourdieu, 1977; Kalpagam, 2000, (a). Such cultural and social norms inhibit women from speaking about their experiences. These norms operate quite strongly in matters of intimacy and family life.

If women have been silenced, subjugated and have themselves internalised their subordinate and unequal position, can they as "speaking subjects" cognise their own oppression and subordinate status? The National Family Health Survey in India found that women from all social classes face some form of domestic violence- their husbands beat them if they do not cook and serve food on time etc., and it also reported that many of the women had responded that it was quite alright if their husbands beat them! Women's non-perception of such oppression is on account of internalisation of oppression as a socially valid norm. So making women narrate their experience is not unproblematic. Although women are likely to report extreme cases of oppression, they may not perceive everyday discrimination or even cognise the possibility of changing social norms. It is therefore necessary to sensitise women which in our present time is being constantly done through various media channels and other forms of education.

Secondly, we need to be aware that women's narration of their experience of oppression may not be a clear black-white story or linear straightforward narration but may be interspersed with reversals, flip-flops and contradictions. Women may fully or partially cognise the power relations and structures and subjectively assess their stakes in making such narrations. Equally such narrations themselves are a process by which women come to their own self understanding.

Thirdly, to whom do the women narrate their experience? Oftentimes women feel that there is nobody to listen to them and the problem is how to get heard. Clearly there are certain moral demands made of the listener and the most important one it seems to me is the ethical one of not negating another's experience just because it does not fit in with either one's own experience or what one wants to listen. Training oneself how to listen is as important as making silenced ones to voice their experiences. Thus speaking and listening require at least two persons around whom an epistemic group could be formed. Inter-subjectivity is an essential component of a feminist epistemology whereby the speaker and listener begin to cognise oppression based on one's experience. Such inter-subjectivity has to be also grounded on a moral equality of the speaker and the listener that binds them as human beings even if otherwise they are differently placed socially, culturally, economically and nationally.

Relations predicated on patriarchal power do not ensure this condition of the moral equality of the speaker and listener which is why patriarchal power fails to cognise how women experience their oppression. Even relations between women could very well replicate patriarchal power under conditions of competition, mistrust or other factors. It is the task of women's activism everywhere to build and cherish such communities of speakers and hearers that seek to extend solidarity to women. Also women's groups in everyday life such as kin members, neighbours and friends, workplace colleagues and so on who do not necessarily identify themselves as feminists more often play this role that is only insufficiently acknowledged by women's studies scholars.

The next issue is whether it is possible to cognise the experiences of all women as a collective. If women's experiences vary and they certainly do by so many determining factors as well as undetermined factors, how is it possible to cognise such a vast terrain of experiences? Here I think *feminist standpoint epistemology* developed by some feminist scholars in the West like Hartsock (2004), Haraway (1988) and others gives some insight. We need to acknowledge that all knowledge is only partial and that from the vantage-point that one is located, we get only a partial understanding of the whole. This is true of the mainstream and male-(centered) knowledge wherein women's experiences and perspectives are not cognised and obliterated. In fact, only by acknowledging that all knowledge is partial and therefore limited, can we begin to understand and lend credibility to the myriad of social movements around the world that as a collective want to privilege their experiences and perspectives-on various issues which they hold, that the authorising powers generally discount. Feminist epistemology is therefore part of social epistemology. Thus we can say that feminist standpoint epistemology shares common ground with all other subaltern and collective action narratives that seek to counterpose the master narratives of authorising powers, be it the group of scientists or the state.

If we now acknowledge that women's experiences can be varying and one who seeks to cognise women's experiences can occupy any one of an infinite number of vantage-points, then it is clear that knowledge of women's experiences could be vast and fragmentary. In fact, this was the criticism that some postmodernist feminist scholars have raised against standpoint feminist epistemology. It is this vast and varied experiences of women upon which women's activism seeks to build solidarity that there are groups and subdivisions and not a single unified women's movement such as the Dalit women's movement, queer movement etc. But it is easy to understand that there is an underlying unity among these subdivisions.

Is there then a way by which this vast and fragmentary knowledge of women's experiences can be amalgamated and integrated into a science or sciences?

This forces us to face head on the next question that philosophers have long addressed-Is experience a valid category of knowledge? Philosophers have spent considerable time on this issue. It is clear that experience that can vary by time and person, although useful to know and can be guide for action, is not as a raw statement of experience considered knowledge but needs to be processed further through scientific, social scientific and humanistic techniques of interpretation and explanation to be constructed as knowledge.

All knowledge is social construction but that does not mean that they can be constructed the way we want. There is a process of validation. Take the case of astronomy and physics. For 14 centuries people believed the Ptolemy system of the earth being at the centre and later the Copernicus heliocentric cosmology of the sun being at the centre was accepted. Although both systems at the times propounded were based on evidence then considered sufficient to base the truth, it is now not possible to revert to the system of Ptolemy. Also, at the time the Copernicus work was published, the Catholic church mounted severe criticism that the findings went against the Holy Scriptures wherein the earth was stationary and at the centre. Today, in the United States the Catholic church is pitted against the American women's movement over the issue of abortion, gay marriages and some aspects of gene research. In the social sciences, there is no doubt a greater flexibility of interpretation than in the physical sciences, but even so the ways of knowledge construction has to be justifiable. Many feminist scholars find mainstream disciplinary knowledge unjustifiable to the extent to which women's experiences are obliterated.

Although there is greater flexibility of interpretation, and acknowledging the social construction of knowledge and ways of producing knowledge, it needs to be noted that sometimes social construction of an entity results in setting up a new hitherto non-existent entity. The most common example is the notion of "majority" and "minority" in a country like India and elsewhere, too. It is only with the statistical enumeration of population through the Census and the momentum of electoral politics that people began to identify themselves as belonging to the 'majority' or 'minority' groups. So, too, in the case of 'caste' that caste identity became politicised. Arguments about the social construction of gender has striven to show that gender differences have been overblown by society far more than the biological difference warrants and that much of the discrimination and the inferior social status of women is on account of that. Gender has therefore emerged as a powerful analytical category for Women's Studies, a category that takes note of the social relation between the sexes as one suffused with power wherein power, encompasses all kinds of power such as economic, social, cultural, political, psychological, linguistic and so on.

Having thus validated "experience" in the construction of knowledge about women and recognising the heterogeneity of women's experience, we are now faced with the question-Is experience the only way of gaining knowledge about women or are there alternative ways of knowing? We are often presented with statistical data, of numbers indicating disparity between men and women on such aspects like employment, wages and income, education etc., from where we get our idea about inequality. We rightly consider such statistical data as pieces of information and transform them into knowledge by making the data amenable to some kind of explanation and interpretation. How far or near is such knowledge to knowledge derived from experience? Statistical frames used for collecting data could be male-biased or gender-blind in the first place and may provide aggregated data that does not help us decipher sex-wise disparities. If they are not gender-blind, somebody already aware of the possible disparities had made them so, such that the disparity could be measured.

Many a time statistical frames are modified and refined so as to adequately capture the real experience for purposes of measurement. The most common example is the Indian Census definition of "work" which by now is well known to scholars in Women's Studies in India. Scholars found that Census under enumerated women workers and sought to examine the reasons for "invisibilising" women's work and then subsequently improved the statistical frame. World-wide feminist economists are now conducting time-use surveys that require close observation and monitoring of how women spend their time, in an effort to improve the data base on women's work such that their work is not undervalued. I am giving this example to tell you that although statistical data may appear to be far away from experience, it is still not completely free from experience, however. Having come to reckon and measure the sex-wise disparity, say on an issue like literacy and education, scholars interested in explaining the gender disparity must move closer to the ground to find out what is happening inside the homes such that girls are not sent to school or drop off from school. The scholar makes a move from an "experience far" context of statistical data to an "experience near" context of listening to what women and girls tell us what is happening inside their homes that prevents them from getting literate and educated.

Thus women's and girls' experiences provide the primary base from which knowledge of women is constructed. We bring a set of explanatory and interpretive methods provided by the social and human sciences to interrogate this experience and also interrogate the methods and theories that underpin this exercise to construct knowledge of women that can be validated and justified.

What about the pedagogy of Women's Studies? By pedagogy we mean the approach to learning and practices of learning. How do people learn about Women? Is Women's Studies a single subject or many subjects? Is it a course and programme of study? At what levels of study in formal and non-formal education are Women's Studies courses introduced? How should Women's Studies be taught? Who are the learners? These are some of the questions that concern the pedagogy of Women's Studies.

I will now concern myself with the disciplinary and inter-disciplinary aspects of Women Studies in the Social Sciences. As mentioned earlier in most of these disciplines, the founding and canonical texts are written by men and espouse the mainstream disciplinary perspective that is also a "malestream" perspective. But feminist scholars have added new perspectives. In the field of economics they have sought to show that "Homoeconomicus" the rational man has indeed got to be a male perspective because women with their familial and nurturing roles can never be the rational utility maximizer the way economic theory posits. The most significant contribution that feminist economics, in my view, has made is the possibility of household-decision modelling that incorporates the power dynamics within the household by bringing in bargaining approach from game theory. Until the early 1980, the household was viewed as a black box into which one could not analytically peep into. Similarly, the varied nuances and ramifications of gender discrimination in labour markets have received world-wide attention. In recent years, human development studies informed by the capabilities and entitlement theory propounded by Amartya Sen has found enthusiastic response from feminist scholars who are now able to approach gender disparities in human development indicators such as income, health, education and so on in an analytically informed way. Some feminist scholars feel that this approach to human development adopts a universalist stance building itself on a human rights approach, and they feel there is no room here for cultural relativism and hence cannot account adequately for cultural differences in the ways of life, and how these ways of life are compelled to change under modernising influences. You can now see how economic issues are gaining from perspectives from other disciplines such as the political theory of human rights and the anthropological notion of culture.

Gender and Development as a sub-discipline of economics has not only added significantly to knowledge about women from developing countries but has played a hugely influential role in policy making at national and international levels. Feminist development scholars from the South countries have successfully demarcated the field and their concerns that are also a consequence of unequal global economic relations as well as the structural conditions of poverty and violence that women face in these postcolonial societies. While their perspectives have grown more nuanced over the years, they have to a great extent succeeded in mainstreaming gender concerns in matters of development policy and governance. The issues they take up are far too numerous to be listed but the more recent concerns have been on the impact of globalisation on women, participatory approaches to development through democratic decentralisation, neoliberal reform agenda on women, gender and governance issues like gender audit of government budgets etc.

Let us now see how the sensibilities of Women's Studies are influencing the disciplines of sociology and anthropology. Kinship studies around which the discipline of Western anthropology constituted itself ignored gender as a factor in kinship relations in society. Today there is concern over gendered kinship and of the roles it plays in social order. Attention is also focussed on the changes in family structures, ideals, norms and values, desires and so on in the family and the reasons thereof and how global forces act on local social institutions like the family and what all these changes entail for women's lives. Similarly, changes in marriage practices and its impact on women of all classes and ages are of concern as well. These studies clearly show that the idealized image of the family may no longer be an analytically sustainable model. Anthropologists also succeeded in bringing biological and social reproduction to the fore from the women's perspective, which has enabled them to occupy certain vanguard positions as debates over new reproductive technologies and genetic research began to snowball in those countries. New sub-disciplines have emerged on account of women's concerns such as the fields of Sexualities and Masculinities and even Men Studies as a complement to Women's Studies. The subjects of anthropology and sociology are a vast ocean and it is impossible for me to list the important arenas wherein gender perspectives have contributed to new insights. Although Women's Studies in the West draws heavily from Psychology especially from the works of Freud and Lacan, Women's Studies in the South countries is not so heavily dependent on psychology and psychoanalysis, although psychologists, too, have contributed to Women's Studies on issues like how women cope with dual or triple roles, how dual career families ensure family well being, issues of domestic violence, women's self-esteem and so on.

In the field of political science, influenced by Women's movements all over the world, political science has spurred renewed concerns over the civic, economic and human rights of women, sought to position women in the debate over the private and public spheres by questioning the public sphere as a male sphere, provided a critique of the functioning of liberal democracies by foregrounding issues of women from minority groups in multicultural societies, extended the arguments for a democratic polity to a democratic society, sought empowerment of women in all political institutions at local, national and international levels, and interrogated war, violence, peace and security issues from feminist perspectives among others.

While feminist historians of a liberal persuasion were keen to retrieve and restore her stories to (His)tory, revisionist histories like the subaltern studies brought forth the study of women's subjectivities and propelled new insights, new histories and new politics of women's resistance. Spivak's classic essay "Can the subaltern speak?" sensitised all feminists to issues of agency and subject even if they otherwise discarded the poststructuralist thought of Foucault and Derrida on whose ideas the essay was thoroughly grounded. Although feminists of all persuasions were always sensitive to issues of power, Foucault's new approach to power made feminists realise on how power constructs subjects which opened avenues for new explorations into the construction of women as subjects and the bio-politics of power.

Postcolonial studies swept Womens Studies like a storm and brought literary scholars into the field of Women's Studies who through nuanced readings of text and context unravelled the hidden positionalities and politics of the subject and theorised difference, hybridty and subjectivity. Postcolonial studies brought heightened sensitivity to how modern state power shaped the domain of law with consequences for women's subject position in the field of law in postcolonial societies. It also sought to establish links to Western thought and ideas while earlier feminists from the South sought a radical break from it. More importantly, postcolonial studies taught feminists that "nation" is not a taken-for-granted category and that nation, citizenship and women need to be theorised conjunctively, once again opening up a rich field of inquiry.

It is now well acknowledged that Women's Studies is an interdisciplinary field of inquiry but even within each disciplines. Women's Studies has opened new avenues of inquiry and provided fresh insights. It is no exaggeration to say that almost on any topic in any of the social sciences it is possible now to write a gender sensitive paper to counter one without it.

Let me now take up curricular issues. Gender sensitivity needs to be introduced in the school curriculum right from the very beginning and this is usually done by avoiding sexist and stereotyped representations of women in textbooks, making girls and women equally represented and visible in pictorial representations in textbooks, not ignoring representation of minority women in textbooks, highlighting the roles played by women be it in history textbooks, civic lessons or in economics, highlighting contributions made by women scientists etc. In various subjects at various classes a chapter could be added highlighting the relevant issues pertaining to women. Of course we need to recognise that sometimes even getting a consensus among the expert group of teachers who authorise such changes can be very difficult, if in fact they are not governed by an overall education policy of the state that brings in these concerns.

At higher education levels in the university, women studies courses are offered within each subject, each subject coming under the purview of a department. At least in Western countries faculty teaching such subjects, say in the Economics Department, often voice anxiety that their male colleagues do not consider their work as real "hard stuff" of algebraic derivations that could get one a Nobel prize. Such tendencies also exist in universities and institutes in other parts of the world and younger faculty caught in the academic rat race of promotions and tenure should be made aware of the stakes involved in this. As in the West, some Indian universities offer BA and MA courses in Women's Studies. It is a basket of courses drawn from different disciplines perhaps drawing faculty to teach them from different departments. While such programmes can be seen as good liberal arts education, it does not ground the student in any single discipline and may have adverse effects on higher research options or in the employment avenue if they do not show proficiency in a single subject. Similarly at the research level M. Phil courses in Women's Studies are available in some universities and a few Ph. D programmes as well. The entrance examination conducted by the University Grants Commission for entry in doctoral research and lectureship has also Women's Studies listed as a subject. However, many scholars doing a doctoral dissertation on a women's issue topic is more likely to be in a non-Women's Studies department, as all departments depending upon the candidates and supervisors interest allow scholars to choose to research on a topic of women's interest.

New disciplines like Media studies, Fashion and Design studies offer much scope to integrate Women's studies into their programmes and so does Management studies as well. In the Indian university set up, they have opened up Women's Studies Centres in some but not all universities to enable interested faculty to take up research on these issues and to enable them to start new courses either independently as a programme of study or integrate it into other departmental studies. Apart from these programmes and centres, India has also started some Women's universities that admit only women students, which perhaps has more to do with promoting women's education. Some of these universities have Women's Studies Centres that claim to have played a leading role in supporting the Women's Studies movement in the country.

Short-term Certificate and Diploma courses on Women's Studies are also offered in Distance Education Open Universities. With the Self-Help Group movement for micro-credit gaining momentum, short-term certificate courses are offered on such topics of relevance to women to participate in these. As education under the Open university system does not require qualifying degrees, women who have just done schooling can also register for these courses.

One can say that very significant efforts have been undertaken to institutionalise Women's Studies in the country. It would now be not so common for male colleagues in a university to raise objections to starting Women's Studies courses although eyebrows would be raised by male faculty and open protest by right-wing factions of student wings and others if a female faculty were to offer a course on Queer Sexuality and Lesbian Rights. Some feminist scholars are of the view that institutionalising Women's Studies has had its drawbacks as it seems to de-politicize the issues and the transformative agendas of the Women's movements are often lost sight of. But in the long run, I think we are better off with these courses than without them, as new thinking is instilled upon a large and young population group. People trained in these programmes could not only work in NGOs and social movements but also provide necessary guidance for the media business as well, which has become a very powerful force in shaping opinion in modern societies.

While all these exist in the formal education set-up, the non-formal education of women, too, is now large and nebulous to categorize. There are many NGOs working for women empowerment focussing on such issues as micro-credit, health, education, rights awareness, environment, and so on. Not only do these NGOs generate local and particular knowledge about women's issues which are sometimes shared by them in national and international forums, these are also used by the NGOs for their own training and educational programmes through which they impart the needed knowledge. Women in these NGO programmes become both generators of knowledge as well as learners themselves. Many of these NGOs have over the years developed their own locally-validated grassroots pedagogies of the oppressed. It is indeed important to generate grassroots feminist theory that would provide a guide for robust local action in ways that integrate and interrogate the interaction of global, national, regional and local factors (Kalpagam, 2002). The recent trend of the institutionalization of the women's movement through the NGOs has also enabled the widespread use of modular training and empowerment methodologies and programmes often developed by international donor agencies and western scholars. This has caused a dilution of the political transformative agendas of the women's movement, so some believe.

What is the relationship of Women's studies to politics? Does politics undergird all exercises in women's studies? Women's Studies have evolved out of the Women's Movements. In India, Women's Studies came on to the scene only from mid-seventies onwards with the massive thrust given by the UN decade for women and the national government endorsing the same. But women's movement existed long before and was an integral part of the nationalist movement. In the two decades following independence, women's movement although not much visible as a national movement played a significant role in the social welfare movement and many remarkable women put up welfare institutions like hospitals and educational institutions which was the need of the hour in the aftermath of independence that endure to this day. Political parties also were not keen to alienate women and had sizeable membership of women. Reports of tribal struggles and the Telengana movement of the peasantry have also recorded participation of women in large numbers. Thus Women's Studies in India and generally elsewhere, too, is organically linked to the women's movements which have been political in nature.

The revival of the women's movement in the seventies and eighties saw much debate and tension between autonomous women's groups in urban centres who took up women's issues cutting across party lines (Kalpagam, 2000,b). Many NGOs working for women in diverse areas also evolved at this juncture. Thus a two-way relationship and flow of ideas was established with overlapping membership between Women's Studies and the women's movement. Many significant policy initiatives such as integrating women's interests in the planning process in India, improvement of data systems, lobbying for appropriate legislations on rape, domestic violence, the politics of the Universal Civil Code and reform of personal laws, establishment of ministries and departments at central and state levels for women-centered issues, bringing gender sensitivity in governance through imparting training to administration officials and so on were simultaneously initiated and pushed through often amidst some opposition.

The late eighties of the last century saw the development of identity politics and the emergence of the Hindu right wing on the national political scene. Women's mobilisation by this political force stood in stark contrast with the centrist and progressive forces that had hitherto occupied the stage of women's movement. Centred around their agenda of cultural nationalism, they espoused the cause of family welfare primarily and the reinforcement of cultural norms that many women find inimical these days. This spurred identity politics further and made the minority Christian and Muslim women's groups to work more within their communities rather than wholeheartedly allying with the progressive factions causing the retrack over the Uniform Civil Code bill. This also brought to the fore the role of religion in women's lives, an issue that progressive movements often tend to ignore. The aggressive strides of the right-wing Women's movement took the progressive groups by total surprise much as it did the political parties at the national level (Kalpagam, 2000, b).

Women's movement got a fillip with the policy of democratic decentralisation that granted women one-third seats in rural governance structures called Panchayats and local governance in urban centres. Tens of thousands of women now sought to become elected representatives and emerged overnight as grassroots leaders. Often illiterate and facing upper-caste resistance if they were Dalits, these women needed to be trained for their new roles as elected representatives of local governance to overseer development works and ensure inclusivity of the development process at the local level. While much euphoria was raised within the women's movement over this new development, it has not shown the needed results over the years as there was no simultaneous devolution of power and finance to the local bodies in some states. Also, both structural poverty and structural violence like caste and communal violence are problems that cannot be solved by just having more women as elected representatives.

While the narration of events so far appears more or less a positive one, taking steps forward, the women's movement has faced the most serious setback regarding one-third seat reservation for women in the central parliament and the state legislatures. although a positive move was made in the parliament recently, it is still a long way from being implemented. Caught up in the Mandal politics of reservations, political parties have not been able to arrive at a consensus on the issue of reservation for OBC (Other Backward Classes), MBC (Most Backward Classes) and SC and ST (Scheduled Castes and Scheduled Tribes) out of this one-third seats allocated for women. Many in the women's movement think that such reservations is an attempt to split the women's movement, while others including powerful women in politics feel that such fragmentation is anyway the present reality. But those supporting such reservation do so not out of concern for women as much as to secure their caste vote-banks. This period has also seen the coming to the fore of Dalit Women's movements in most parts of the country, either as autonomous movements or as part of a political party focussing on issues like land rights and caste atrocities.

Women's Studies have made substantial contributions towards all these issues first by identifying the issues, providing analysis and examining the effects of policy etc. They have also taken up other issues of pressing concern, which are also political such as the effects of globalisation and the neoliberal reform agendas on women. Women's Studies is by and large influenced by the transformative goals of the women's movement in that it hopes to change women's lives for the better. It also needs to be noted that there is no consensus among feminists and others of doing so. But there are many other topics, issues and subjects that Women's Studies take up wherein politics is not so easily visible. Take for instance the field of performing arts. Feminism inspired concerns had led eminent dancers like the late Chandralekha from Chennai to experience new dance forms, to experiment with body movements and rhythms for women to gain expressive freedom. Women artists, poets and writers are also engaged in this struggle of trying to break free from the conventions of genre to gain expressive freedom. Women have always done this, to render folk narratives in ways more appealing to them as research on the varied versions of the Ramayana epic that circulates indicate so. Thus Women's Studies and the women's movements as a modernist enterprise relates to ways of knowing and doing that enables women to enlarge the domains of freedom for the full development of their personalities and self, and to lead fulfilling lives. And needless to say it is a pluralist agenda for there can be many ways of achieving it.

Notes

1. This paper was presented at an international workshop organized by WERC in Colombo, Sri Lanka on December 5-6, 2009. I am especially thankful to Selvy Thiruchandran for her

comments and the opportunity to participate in the workshop. I thank the workshop participants for their comments that helped me to revise the paper.

References

Bourdieu, P. 1977, *Outline of a Theory of Practice,* (Cambridge: Cambridge University Press).

Haraway, Donna 1988, 'Situated Knowledges: The Science Question in Feminism and the Privilege of Partial Perspective', *Feminist Studies*, Vol. 14, No. 3, Autumn, pp. 575-599.

Hartsock, Nancy C.M. 2004, 'The Feminist Standpoint: Developing the Ground for a Specifically Feminist Historical Materialism', in Sandra Harding and Merrill B. Hintikka (eds), *Discovering Reality: Feminist Perspectives on Epistemology, Metaphysics, Methodology and Philosophy of Science*, (Netherlands, Springer).

Kalpagam, U. 2002, 'Perspectives for a Grassroots Feminist Theory', *Economic and Political Weekly,* Vol. 37, No.47, (Nov. 23-29), pp. 4686-4693.

Kalpagam, U. 2000, a 'Life Experiences, Resistance and Feminist Consciousness', *Indian Journal of Gender Studies*, Vol. 7, No. 2, pp.167-184.

Kalpagam, U. 2000, b 'The Women's Movement in India: New Agendas and Old Problems', *Feminist Studies*, Vol. 26, No. 3, Autumn, pp. 645-660.

List of Contributors

U. Kalpagam is professor at the G.B. Pant Social Science Institute, Allahabad. She is both an economist and an anthropologist and has published extensively on gender issues. She trained in Economics at IIT, Kanpur and in Anthropology at the New School for Social Research, New York. She is the author of *Labour and Gender* (Sage, 1994) and has co-edited *Labour and Poverty, Development and Empowerment, Rural Women in South Asia* and *Rural Women and Development in India.* Two books authored by her *Globalisation and Neoliberalism in India: Gender Perspectives* and *Gender and Development in India* will soon be published. Her research interests include Gender Studies, Labour Economics, Urban Studies, Colonial and Postcolonial Studies.

Maitrayee Chaudhuri is professor of Sociology with the Centre for the Study of Social Systems, Jawaharlal Nehru University, New Delhi. She was earlier the Director of the Women's Studies Programme, JNU. Her areas of interest are gender, culture, media and pedagogy. Her works include *The Indian Women's Movement: Reform and Revival*, *The Practice of*

Sociology (ed.), *Feminism in India* (ed.), and *Sociology in India: Institutional and Intellectual Practices* (ed.)

Fatima Burnad Nadesan is an activist and President of Society for Rural Education and Development (SRED). She has been working among the Dalits, Landless and Tribal Women for the past 35 years. She has promoted a state level forum, Tamil Nadu Women's Forum (TNWF), for the purpose of bringing women's groups as well as human rights groups together. She has also promoted Tamil Nadu Dalit Women's Movement (TNDWM) and is now working to strengthen Dalit women leadership. She is coordinating the activities of TNDWM/ TNWF / SRED. She has been a trainer and a resource person at various seminars / workshops. She has studied in the US and has been Research Fellow at the IDS, Sussex in the UK. She is serving as Board member in many international organizations such as AWID-Association of Women in Development, and IMADR-International Movement Against Discrimination and Racism, Steering Council Member of Pesticide Action Network Asia Pacific (PANAP), Core Committee member for Asia with DCA-Dan Church Aid -Denmark.

Vibhuti Patel is professor and head of the University Department of Economics and Director, Department of Post Graduate Studies and Research, SNDT Women's University, Mumbai and holds a Doctorate in Economics. She is an Expert Committee member of School of Gender and Development Studies for IGNOU, member of Advisory Board of Department of Women's Studies of NCERT and member of the subgroup on "Gender, Micro Finance and local Self Government Bodies" for the 11th Five Year Plan,

Government of India. She has published extensively on gender issues nationally and internationally.

Sumita Parmar is professor in the Department of English and Modern European Languages in the University of Allahabad. She has done post doctoral work in the University of California, Berkeley on African American women writers. She is interested in Women's Writings and Feminism and has published various articles on these subjects. She is the Director of the Centre of Women's Studies in the University. She edits a bi-annual journal *Journal of Women's Studies* which was launched in 2007.

Subhadra Mitra Channa is professor of Anthropology at the University of Delhi. She was a Charles Wallace Fellow and a Visiting Professor to MSH, Paris, Fulbright visiting lecturer to USA and a Visiting Professor in 2008-9 to University of South Carolina, USA. She has written about fifty scholarly papers and is author/editor of four books. She was the President of the Indian Anthropological Association and currently is editor of the *Indian Anthropologist*. She also chairs the Commission on the Anthropology of Women (IUAES).

Rehana Ghadially is retired professor of Psychology in the Department of Humanities and Social Sciences at the Indian Institute of Technology, Mumbai. She is a recipient of several international fellowships and has published in national and international journals. She has edited two books published by Sage Publications, New Delhi: *Women in Indian Society: A Reader* (1989) and *Urban Women in Contemporary India: A Reader* (2007). Her research and teaching interests focus on Gender Issues and Stress Management.

Index

N

U

V

W